Éditions DIASPORAS NOIRES

www.diasporas-noires.com

©Emmanuel Ngombet 2020

ISBN digital version : 9782490931125

ISBN printed version : 9782490931132

Date of digital publication : June 22, 2020

.

Emmanuel NGOMBET DITUNGA OTSARO

The United African States

The African Federal State

Essay

Collection Savoirs

English translation by Josephine Ndiaye

SOMMAIRE

Foreword

The Bell is ringing, the tipping time is on. The world is changing and a world of possibilities is right there, just before us. The Bell is ringing. Time (Tangu ifoueni) to create an African federal state has come.

The Bell (Ngungâ) is also ringing to RE-UNITE this fractured Africa and RE-ASSEMBLE this black skin, that has been scattered away all over the world

Reassemble (Konguela) again towards the center (n'zita dia n'za), I named Kongo, presently Angola territory along with the two Congo, DRC (the Democratic Republic of the Congo), and CR (the Republic of Congo, adding to that the Middle Congo, up to the Great Lakes.

Re-unite the lands of Bornou, Monomotapa, Ethiopia, and Sonrhaï.

Reach the tipping point means ending the existence of all microstates, as defined at the Berlin conference and designed at the time of independence.

Time has come to create the United States of Africa (African United States) to accomplish the peoples' will.

Our heads of states continue to be passive regarding this situation in which they are as powerful kings, they find themselves quite content within the fixed currency pattern with euro (or dollar or yuan).

With this fixed parity, monetary inflation is being maintained, although it does not lead to economic growth, while a necessary condition for any development.

The point is that by doing so, they do not perceive or feign to ignore that times have changed. This sort of extension of the Cfa franc to all the countries of Western Africa is felt like a burden by the young African people who see it like, not only an extension of French colonization but that of Europe all over Africa.

Although they were set free, the former slaves do not wish to stay too far from the master's plant comfort and would rather propose their abundant and affordable working abilities.

The birth of a federal state will end the debate, as the use of a single currency is a vital condition to its very existence.

Preface

For the last twenty years, I have been investing all of my energy into freeing the black Man from mental slavery caused by the violence of both colonization and holy wars (crusades and Jihad) which led Negro-African nations to be dominated through the influence of Christian and Islamic religions.

Drones (everything is under surveillance and tracked by foreigners), laboratory imported diseases (Aids and Ebola, inoculated through vaccines) nuclear plants (turnkey contracts and long-term credits) being as many factors leading to the ownership of our lands with the blessings of our leaders.

The brain drain to the Occident and the extinguishment of our elites by the same predators and by ourselves are as many factors concurring to a new form of slavery and even to the genocide of the Black African Man.

I have been requested, through this book, to catch the spirit leading into the process of creation of the United States of Africa, with the help of both the civil society and the African citizens.

The United States of Africa (USOA) flag, based on the starry Gold Spiral, with rainbow colors, the crest with the eye of Horus, the refrain of the Union Hymn, sung by the citizens placed in position 11 of the "Kemet Sun Salutation" have suggested me a new world of possibilities for Africa. This USOA flag is an amazing work of art.

The constitution of gold reserves, which profitability will be increased through private businesses, the soft water project that will be taken through the arid lands of the continent, the project of construction of the replica of the SAQQARA pyramid (meant to be the poles of both knowledge and university), has convinced me once and for all, that Africa is meant to be the desirable future of humanity, as she is already said to be the cradle of mankind.

Arsène Francoeur NGANGA

Research-Professor in History/Marien NGOUABI University

Presently (2019-2020) studying in writing house at Brown University, Rhode Island the USA

1. African States of the continent and Overseas Territories

The citizen and the civil society will drive to the creation of an embryo of the African federal state, of African states, before being extended to the people from African descent from Overseas.

African people should from now on, be on the move, stop complaining and start challenging, stop incantation and, take action and, start anticipation.

In 2020, the civil society and the citizens are going to discuss the feasibility and the opportunity to proceed, seriously, to the symbolic creation of the United States of Africa, the United African States, U.A.S.

African United States/UAS will make the debate concerning the microstates criterion convergence irrelevant because the adoption of the single currency is the backbone and foundation leading to the very existence of this nations' union.

Can we anticipate on our common future?

Initialize the collection of public and private savings (that of the citizen becoming a shareholder/actor) to gather the gold and currency reserves, needed for the creation of the single currency of the African federal State.

Define our own "backbones and foundations", both politically and economically speaking, to get to the union of African states

2. Constitution of the United States of Africa

PREAMBLE

We, People of the 55 current countries of Africa (South Africa, Algeria, Angola, Benin, Botswana, Burkina Faso, Burundi, Cameroon, Cape-Verde, the Central Africa Republic, Comoros, the Republic of Congo, the Democratic Republic of Congo, Ivory Coast, Djibouti, Egypt, Erythrea, Gabon, the Gambia, Ghana, Bissau-Guinea, Guinea Conakry, Equatorial Guinea, Kenya, Lesotho, Liberia, Lybia, Madagascar, Malawi, Mali, Morocco, Mauricia, Mauritania, Mozambique, Namibia, Niger, Nigeria, Uganda, Rwanda, Sao Tome and Principe, Senegal, Seychelles, Sierra Leone, Somalia, Somaliland, Sudan, South Sudan, Swaziland, Tanzania, Chad, Togo, Tunisia, Zambia, Zimbabwe), to form a more perfect Union, establish Justice, insure domestic Tranquility, provide for the common defense, promote the general Welfare, and secure the Blessings of Liberty to ourselves and our Posterity, do ordain and establish this Constitution for the United States of Africa.

ARTICLE ONE

Section 1.

All legislative Powers herein granted shall be vested in a Congress of The United States of Africa which shall consist of a Senate and a House of Representatives.

Section 2.

The House of Representatives shall be composed of members chosen every third year by the people of the several States and the Electors in each State shall have the qualification requisite for Electors of the most numerous Branch of the State Legislature.

No Person shall be a Representative who shall not have attained the age of twenty five years, and been seven years a Citizen, of the United States of Africa, and who shall not, when elected, be a inhabitant of that State in which he shall be chosen.

Representatives and direct taxes shall be apportioned among the different states which may be included within this Union according to their respective numbers. Census (through terminals) shall be conducted within two years after the first meeting of the Congress and within subsequent term of ten years, in such manner as they shall by Law direct.

When vacancies happen in the Representation from any State, the Executive Authority thereof shall issue Writs of Election to fill such vacancies.

The House of Representatives shall choose their Speaker (rotating presidency according to states alphabetical order) and other Officers (15, one by State) ; and shall have the sole power of Impeachment before the Senate.

Section 3.

The Senate of the United States of Africa shall be composed of two Senators from each State, chosen by the Legislature thereof for six years and each Senator will have one vote. Immediately after they shall be assembled in consequence of the first Election, they shall be divided as equally as may be into three classes. The seats of the Senators of the first class shall be vacated at the expiration of the second year, of the second class at the expiration of the fourth year, so that one third may be chosen every second year ; and if vacancies happen by resignation or otherwise, during the recess of the the legislature of any State, the Executive thereof may make temporary appointments until the next meeting of the legislature which shall then fill such vacancies.

No person shall be a Senator who shall not have attained the age of thirty years, and been nine years a citizen of the

United States of Africa, and who shall not, when elected, be an inhabitant of that State for which he shall be chosen.

The Vice President of the United State of Africa shall be President of the Senate, but shall have no vote, unless they be equally divided.

The Senate shall choose their other officers, and also a President pro tempore, in the absence of the Vice President of the United States of Africa, or when he shall exercise the Office of President of the United States of Africa.

The Senate will have the sole power to try all Impeachment. When sitting for that purpose, they shall be on oath or affirmation. When the President of the United States of Africa is tried, the Chief Justice shall preside. And No person shall be convicted without the concurrence of two thirds of the members present.

Judgment in cases of Impeachment shall not extend further than to removal from office, and disqualification to hold and enjoy any office of honor, trust or profit under the United States of Africa; but the party convicted shall nevertheless be liable and subject indictment trial, judgment and punishment according to Law.

Section 4.

The times, places and manner of holding Elections for senators and representatives, shall be prescribed in each State by the Legislature thereof, but the Congress may at any time by Law, make or alter such regulations, except as to the place of choosing Senators.

The Congress shall assemble at least once in every year, on the first monday in December, unless they shall by Law appoint a different day.

Section 5.

Each House shall be the judge of the Elections, Returns and Qualifications of its own members, and a majority of each shall constitute the Quorum to do business, but a smaller number may adjourn from day to day and may be authorized to compel the attendance of absent members, in such manners and under such penalties as each House may provide.

Each House may determine the rules of its proceedings, punish its members for disorderly behavior, and with the concurrence of two-thirds, expel a member.

Each House shall keep a Journal of its proceedings, and from time to time publish the same, excepting such parts as may in their judgment require secrecy, and the yeas and nays of the members of either House on any question shall, at the desire of one fifth of those present, be entered on the Journal.

Neither House, during the Session of Congress, shall, without the consent of the other, adjourn for more than three days, not to any other place than that in which the two Houses shall be sitting.

Section 6.

The Senators and Representatives shall receive a compensation for their services, to be ascertained by Law and paid out of the Treasury of the United States of Africa.

They shall in all cases, except treason, felony and breach of the Peace, be privileged from arrest during their attendance at the Session of their respective Houses, and in going to and returning from the same; and for any speech or debate in either House, they shall not be questioned in any other place.

No Senator or Representative shall, during the time for which he was elected, be appointed to any civil office under the authority of the United States of Africa which shall have been created, or the emoluments whereof shall have been increased during such time, and no person holding any office under the United States of Africa, shall be a member of either House during his continuance in office.

Section 7.

All bills for raising revenue shall originate in the House of Representatives; but the Senate may propose or concur with amendments as on other Bills.

Every Bill which shall have passed the House of Representatives and the Senate, shall, before it become a Law, be presented to the President of the United States of Africa; if he approves he shall sign it, but if not he shall return it with his objections to that House in which it shall have originated, who shall enter the objections at large on their Journal, and proceed to reconsider it. If after such reconsideration, two thirds of that House shall agree to pass the Bill, it shall be sent, together with the objections, to the other House, by which it shall likewise be reconsidered, and if approved by two thirds of that House, it shall become a Law. But in all such cases the votes of both Houses shall be determined by Yeas and Nays, and the names of the persons voting for and against the Bill shall be entered on the Journal of each House respectively. If any Bill shall not been returned by the President within ten days (Sundays excepted) after it shall have been presented to him, the same shall be a Law, in like manner as if he had signed it, unless the Congress by their adjournment prevent its return, in which case it shall not be a Law.

Every order, resolution, or vote to which the concurrence of the Senate and House of Representatives may be necessary (except on a question of Adjournment) shall be presented to the President of the United States of Africa, and before the same shall take effect, the Senate and House of Representatives, according to the rules and limitations prescribed in the case of a Bill.

Section 8.

The Congress shall have power :

To lay and collect taxes, duties, Imposts and Exercises,

To pay the debts and provide for the common defence and General Welfare of the United States of Africa but all duties, imposts and exercises shall be uniform throughout the United States of Africa;

Borrow money on the credit of the United States of Africa ;

Regulate commerce with Foreign Nations, and among the several states;

To establish an uniform rule of naturalization and uniform Laws on the subject of bankruptcies throughout The United States of Africa;

To coin money, regulate the value thereof, and of foreign coin, and fix the standard of weights and measures;

To provide for the punishment of counterfeiting the securities and current coin of the United States of Africa ;

To establish Post Offices and Post Roads;

To promote the progress of Science and useful Arts, by securing for limited times to authors and inventors the exclusive right to their respective writings and discoveries;

To constitute Tribunals inferior to the Supreme Court;

To define and punish Piracies and Felonies committed on the high Seas, and Offenses against the Law of Nations;

To negotiate as much as possible in order to avoid war,

To grant letters of marque and reprisal, and make rules concerning captures on land and water;

To raise and support armies, but no appropriation of money to that use shall be for a longer term than two years;

To create and maintain a Navy, that can be used for any purpose, including environmental problems;

To make rules for the government and regulation of the land and naval forces ;

To provide for calling forth the Militia to execute the laws of the Union, suppress insurrections and repel invasions;

To organize a one year (twelve months) military reserve-style model in which civic service would provide young people who have attained the legal age of 18, all activities including army, health, education, agriculture, public interest cleaning);

To provide for organizing, arming and disciplining the Militia, and for governing such part of them as may be employed the Service of the United States of Africa, reserving to the States respectively, the appointment of the officers, and the authority of training the Militia according to the discipline prescribed by Congress ;

To exercise exclusive legislation in all cases whatsoever, over such district (not exceeding ten miles square) as may by cession of particular States, and the acceptance of Congress, become the seat of the government of the United states of Africa, and to exercise like authority over places purchased by the consent of the legislature of the state in which the same shall be, for the erection of forts, magazines, arsenals, dockyards and other needful buildings;

And to make all laws which shall be necessary and proper for carrying into execution the foregoing powers, and all other powers vested by the Constitution in the Government of the United States of Africa, or in any department or Officer thereof.

Section 9.

The migration or importation of such persons as any of the states now existing shall think proper to admit, shall not be prohibited by the Congress, but a tax or duty may be imposed on such importation not exceeding ten Dollars for each person. The privilege of the Writs of Habeas Corpus shall not be suspended, unless when in cases of rebellion or invasion the public safety may require it.

No Bill of Attainder or ex post facto law shall be passed.

No capitation, or other direct tax shall be laid, unless in proportion to the census herein before directed to be taken.

No tax or duty shall be laid on articles exported from any state.

No preferences shall be given by any regulation of commerce or revenue to the ports of one state over those of another nor shall vessels bound to, or fro, one state be obliged to enter, clear, or pay duties in another.

No money shall be drawn from the Treasury, but in consequence of appropriations made by law; and a regular statement and account of the receipts and expenditures of all public money shall be published from time to time.

No title of nobility shall be granted by the United States of Africa ; and no person holding any office of profit or trust under them, shall, without the consent of the Congress, accept of any present, emolument, office, or title, of any kind whatever, from any king, prince or foreign state.

Section 10.

No state shall enter into any Treaty, Alliance, or Confederation, grant letters of Marque and Reprisal; coin money, emit bills of credit, make anything but gold and silver coin a tender in payment of debts; pass any bill of Attainder, ex post facto law, or law impairing the obligation of contracts, or grant any title of nobility.

No state shall, without the consent of the Congress, lay any taxes or duties on imports or exports, except what may be absolutely necessary for executing its inspection laws; and the net produce of all duties and imposts, laid by any state on imports or exports, shall be for the use of the Treasury, of the United States of Africa, and all such laws shall be subject to the revision and control of the Congress.

No state shall, without the consent of Congress, lay any duty of Tonnage, keep troops, or ships of war in time of peace, enter into any agreement of compact with another state, or with a foreign power, or engage war, unless actually invaded, or in such imminent danger as will not admit of delay.

ARTICLE II

Section 1.

The executive Power shall be vested in the President of The United States of Africa. He shall hold his office during the term of four years, and together with the Vice President chosen for the same term, be elected as follows :

Presidency shall alternate by state on the basis of alphabetical order state list. Vice-Presidency shall also alternate on the other way round.

The thirteen other positions according to their Importance in the protocol order, will be submitted to this rotation, so that each state will be represented at the head of federal organization.

The fifteen top executives shall be elected by direct universal suffrage, through terminals. Votes shall take place during 48 hours NON-STOP, immediately counted and automatically compiled to the organ in charge of publishing results.

Each state may organize primary elections under the same principle of alternate rotation, in order to choose their own candidates whose number shall not exceed three, the candidates shall be elected by universal suffrage for the sought position.

Each executive, in charge of one the highest federal position, (President, Vice President, Speaker at the Congress,...), that is a candidate to his own position or to Another position, shall resign prior to the beginning of the following campaign.

To this end he shall be replaced by the deputy under Protocol order. No person is allowed to campaign while being in office, nor use in any way the state means for his own or personal interest. All candidates are equal in rights and citizenship.

Section 2.

The president shall be commander in chief of the Army and the Navy of the United States of Africa, of the militia of the several states, when called into the actual service of federal states; he may require the opinion in writing, of the principal Officer in each of the executive departments, upon any subject related to the duties of their respective offices and he shall have power to grant reprieves and pardon for offenses against the United States, except in cases of « Impeachment ».

He shall have power, by and with the advice and consent of the Senate, to make treaties, provide two thirds of the

Senators present concur; and he shall nominate, and by and with the advice and consent of the Senate, shall Appoint ambassadors, other public ministers and consuls, Judges of the Supreme Court, and all other officers of the United States of Africa, whose appointments are not herein otherwise provided for, and which shall be Established by law.

But the Congress may by law vest the appointment of such inferior officers, as they think proper, in the President alone, in the courts of law, or in the Heads of departments.

The president shall have power to fill up all vacancies that May happen during the recess of the Senate by granting Commissions which shall expire at the end of their session.

Section 3.

The President shall from time to time give the Congress information of the state of the Union and recommend their consideration such measures as he shall judge necessary and expedient; he may, on extraordinary occasions, convene both Houses, or either of them, and in case of disagreement between them, with respect to the time of adjournment, he may adjourn them to such time as he shall think proper; he shall receive Ambassadors and other public ministers. He shall take care that the laws be faithfully executed and shall Commission all athe officers of the United States of Africa.

Section 4.

The President, Vice President and all civil officers of the United States of Africa shall be removed from office on Impeachment for, and conviction of, treason, bribery or other high crimes and misdemeanors.

ARTICLE III

Section 1.

The Judicial power of the United States of Africa shall be vested in one Supreme Court, and in such inferior Courts as the Congress may from time to time ordain and establish. The Judges, both of the Supreme and inferior Courts, shall hold their offices during good behavior, and shall, at stated times receive for their services a compensation which shall not be diminished during their continuance in office.

Section 2.

The judicial power shall extend to all cases, in law and equity, arising under this Constitution, the laws of the United States of Africa and treaties made, or which shall be made under their authority, to all cases affecting Ambassadors, other public Ministers and Consuls; to all cases of admiralty and maritime jurisdiction; to controversies to which the

United States of Africa shall be a party; to controversies between two or more States; between a State and citizens of another state; between citizens of different states, between citizens of the same state claiming lands under grants of different states, and between states, or the citizen thereof, and foreign states, citizens or subjects.

In all cases affecting ambassadors, other public Ministers and Consuls, and those in which a State shall be party, the Supreme Court shall have original jurisdiction.

In all other cases before mentioned, the Supreme Court shall have the Appellate Jurisdiction, both as to law and fact, with such exceptions, and un der regulations as the Congress shall make.

The trial of all crimes, except in cases of impeachment, shall be by Jury; and such trial shall be held in the state where the said crimes shall have been committed; but when not committed within any state, the trial shall be at such place or places as the Congress may by law have directed.

Section 3.

Treason against the United States of Africa, shall consist only in levying war against them, or in adhering to their enemies, giving them aid and comfort.

No person shall be convicted of treason unless on the testimony of two witnesses to the same overt act, or on confession in open court.

The Congress shall have power to declare punishment of treason, but no attainder of treason shall work corruption of blood, or forfeiture except during the Life of the person attainted.

ARTICLE IV

Section 1.

Full faith and Credit shall be given in each state to the public acts, records, and judicial proceedings of every other state. And the Congress may by general laws prescribe the manner in with such acts, records and proceedings shall be proved, and the effect thereof.

Section 2.

The citizens of each state shall be entitled to all privileges and immunities of citizens in the several states.A person charged in any State with treason, felony, or other crimes, who shall flee from justice, and be found in another state, shall on demand of the Executive Authority of the state from which he fled, be delivered up, to be removed to the state having jurisdiction of the crime.

No person held to Service or Labour in one State, under the laws thereof, escaping into another, shall, in consequences of any law or regulation therein, be discharged from such service or labour, but shall be delivered up on claim of the Party to whom such Service or Labour may be due.

Section 3.

New states may be admitted by the Congress into this Union; but no new state shall be formed or erected within the jurisdiction of any other state, nor any state formed by the junction of two or more states, without the consent of the legislature of the states concerned as well as of the Congress.

The Congress shall have power to dispose of and make all needful rules and regulations respecting the territory or other property belonging to the United States of Africa, and nothing in this Constitution shall be so construed as to prejudice any claims of the United States of Africa, or of any particular state.

Section 4.

The United States of Africa shall guarantee to every state in this Union a republican form of government, and shall protect each of them against invasion; and on application of the legislature, or of the Executive (when the legislature cannot be convened) against domestic violence.

ARTICLE V

The Congress, whenever two thirds of both Houses shall deem it necessary, shall propose amendments to this Constitution, or, on the application of the Legislatures of two thirds of the several states, shall call a convention for proposing amendments, which in either case, shall be valid to all intents and purposes, as part of this Constitution, when ratified by the legislatures of three fourths of the several states, or by conventions, in three fourths thereof, as the one or the other mode of ratification may be proposed by the Congress, provided that no amendments shall in any manner affect the first and fourth clauses in the ninth section of the first article; and that no state, without its consent, shall be deprived of its equal suffrage in the Senate.

ARTICLE VI

All debts contracted and engagements entered into, before the adoption of this Constitution, shall be as valid against the United States of Africa under this Constitution as under the Confederation.

This Constitution, and the laws of the United States of Africa which shall be made in pursuance thereof; and all treaties made, or which shall be made, under the Authority of the United States of Africa, shall be the supreme Law of the Lan; and the judges in every State shall be bound thereby, anything in the Constitution or Laws of any State to the contrary notwithstanding.

The Senators and Representatives before mentioned, and the members of the several states legislatures, and all executive and judicial officers, both of the United States of Africa and of the several states, shall be bound by Oath or Affirmation, to support this Constitution; but no religious Test shall ever be required as a qualification to any office or public trust under the United States of Africa.

ARTICLE VII

The Ratification of the Convention of nine States out of fifteen, shall be sufficient for the establishment of this constitution between the States so ratifying the same.

Done in Convention by the Unanimous Consent of the Congress

In Witness whereof

We have hereunto subscribed our Names

SUGGESTED AMENDMENTS

ARTICLE I

Congress shall make no law respecting an establishment of religion, or prohibiting the free exercise thereof; or abridging the freedom of speech, or of the press, or the right of the people peaceably to assemble, and to petition the Government for a redress of grievances.

ARTICLE II

A well regulated Militia, being necessary to the security of a free state, the right of the people to keep and bear arms, for their own defence shall be determined by the Public force under the terms of the rule of law.

ARTICLE III

No soldier shall, in time of peace, be quartered in any House, without the consent of the owner, nor in time of war, but in a manner to be prescribed by law.

ARTICLE IV

The right of the people to be secure in their persons, houses, papers, and effects, against unreasonable searches and seizures, shall both be violated, and no warrants shall be issued but upon probable cause, supported by Oath or affirmation, and particularly describing the place to be searched, and the persons or things to be seized.

ARTICLE V

No person shall be held to answer for a capital, or otherwise infamous crime, unless on a presentment or indictment of a Grand Jury, except in cases arising in the land or naval forces, or in the Militia, when in actual service in time of war or public danger; nor shall any person be subject for the same offence to be twice put in jeopardy of life or limb; nor shall be compelled in any criminal case to be a witness against himself, nor be deprived of life, liberty, or property, without due process of law; nor shall private property be taken for public use, without just compensation.

ARTICLE VI

In all prosecutions, the accused will enjoy the right to a speedy and public trial, by an impartial jury of the state and district wherein the crime shall have been committed, which district shall have been previously ascertained by law, and to be informed of the nature and cause of the accusation; to be confronted with the witnesses against him; to have compulsory process for obtaining witnesses in his favor, and to have the assistance of Counsel for his defense.

ARTICLE VII

In suits at common law, where the value in controversy shall exceed twenty dollars, the right of trial shall be preserved, and no fact tried by a jury, shall be otherwise re-examined in any court of the United States of Africa, than according to the rules of the common law.

ARTICLE VIII

Excessive bail shall not be required, nor excessive fines imposed, nor cruel and unusual punishments inflicted.

ARTICLE IX

The enumeration in the Constitution, of certain rights, shall not be construed to den or disparage others retained by the people.

ARTICLE X

The powers not delegated to the United States of Africa by the constitution, nor prohibited by it to the states, are reserved to the States respectively, or to the people.

ARTICLE XI

The judicial power of the United States shall not be construed to extend to any suit in law or equity, commenced or prosecuted against one of the United States of Africa by citizens of another state, or by citizens of subjects of any foreign state.

ARTICLE XII

The electors shall meet in their respective states, and vote by ballot for President and Vice President, one of whom, at least, shall not be an inhabitant of the same state with themselves; they shall name in their ballots the person voted for as President, and in distinct ballots the person voted for as Vice President and of the number of votes for each, which lists they shall sign and certify, and transmit sealed to the seat of the government of the United States of Africa, directed to the President of the Senate.The President of the Senate shall, in the presence of the Senate and the House of Representatives, open all the certificates and the votes shall be counted. The person having the greatest number of votes for President, shall be the President, if such number be a majority, then from the persons having the highest numbers not exceeding three on the list of those voted for as President, the House of Representatives shall choose immediately, by ballot, the President but in choosing the President, the votes shall be taken by states, the representation from each state having one vote; a quorum for this purpose shall consist of a member or members from two-thirds of the states, and a majority of all the states shall be necessary to a choice. And if the House of Representatives shall not choose a President whenever the right of choice shall devolve upon them, before the fourth day of March next following, then the Vice President shall act as President, as in the case of the death or other constitutional disability of the President.

The person having the greatest number of votes as Vice President, shall be the Vice President, if such number be a majority of whole number of electors appointed, and if no person have a majority, then from the two highest numbers on the list, the Senate shall choose the Vice President; a quorum for the purpose shall consist of 24, which shall represent two-thirds of the whole number of senators, and a majority of the whole number shall be necessary to a choice.

But no person constitutionally inelegible to the office of President shall be eligible to that of Vice President of the United States of Africa.

ARTICLE XIII

Section 1.

Neither slavery nor involuntary servitude, except as a punishment for crime whereof the party shall have been duly convicted, shall exist within the United States of Africa, or any place subject to their jurisdiction. The federal state shall investigate on every suspicious case of servitude especially of youngsters under the age of majority, that may have been sold as payment for incurred family debts.

ARTICLE XIV

Section 1.

All persons born or naturalized in the United States of Africa, and subject to the jurisdiction thereof, are citizens of the United States of Africa and of the

State wherein they reside. No state shall make or enforce any law which abridge the privileges or immunities of citizens of the United States of Africa; nor shall

any state deprive any person of life, liberty, or property, without due process of law; nor deny to any person within its jurisdiction the equal protection of the laws.

Section 2.

No person shall be a Senator or Representative in Congress, or elector of President and Vice President, or hold any office, civil or military, under the United States of Africa, or under any state, who, having previously taken an oath, as a member of Congress, or as an officer of the United States of Africa, or as a member of any state legislature, or as an executive or judicial officer of any state, to support the

constitution of the United States of Africa, shall have engaged in insurrection or rebellion against the same, or given aid or comfort to the enemies thereof. But Congress may vote of two thirds of each House, remove such disability.

Section 3.

The validity of the public debt of the United States of Africa, authorized by law, including debts incurred for payments of pensions and bounties for services in suppressing.

But neither the United States of Africa nor any state shall assume or pay any debt or obligation incurred in aid of insurrection or rebellion against the United States of Africa, or any claim for the loss or emancipation of any slave; but all such debts, obligations and claims shall be held illegal and void.

ARTICLE XV

Section 1.

The right of citizens of the United States of Africa to vote shall not be denied or abridged by the United States or by any state on account of race, color, or previous condition of servitude.

ARTICLE XVI

The Congress shall have power to lay and collect taxes on incomes, from whatever source derived, without apportionment among the several states, and without regard to any census or enumeration.

ARTICLE XVII

Section 1.

The Senate of the United States of Africa shall be composed of two Senators from each state, elected by the people thereof, for six years through terminal and confirmed by ballot.

Section 2.

When vacancies happen in the representation of any state in the Senate, the executive authority of such state shall issue writs of election to fill such vacancies provided that the legislature of any state may empower the executive thereof to make temporary appointments until the people fill the vacancies by election as the legislature may direct.

Section 3.

This amendment shall not be so construed as to affect the election or term of any senator chosen before it becomes valid as part of the Constitution.

ARTICLE XVIII

The right of citizens of the United States of Africa to vote shall not be denied or abridged by the United States of Africa or by any state on account of gender.

Congress shall have power to enforce this article by appropriate legislation.

ARTICLE XIX

Section 1.

The terms of the President and Vice President shall end at noon on the 20th day of May, and the terms of Senators and Representatives at noon on the third day of May, of the years in which such terms would have ended if this article had not been ratified; and the terms of their successors shall then begin.

Section 2.

The Congress shall assemble at least once in every year, and such meeting shall begin at noon on the third day of May, unless they shall by law appoint a different day.

Section 3.

If, at the time fixed for the beginning of the term of the President, the President elect shall have died, the Vice President elect shall become President.

If a President shall not have been chosen before the time fixed for the beginning of this term, or if the President elect shall have failed to qualify, then the Vice President elect shall act as President until a President shall have qualified, declaring who shall then act as President, or in the manner in which one who is to act shall be selected, and such person shall act accordingly until a President or Vice President shall have qualified.

Section 4.

The Congress may by law provide for the case of the death of any of the persons from whom the House of Representatives may choose a President whenever the right of choice shall have devolved upon them.

ARTICLE XX

Section 1.

No person shall be elected to the office of the President more than twice, and no person who has held the office of President, or acted as President, for more than two years of a term to which some other person was elected President shall be elected to the office of the President more than once. But this article shall not apply to any person holding the office of President, when this article was proposed by the Congress, and shall not prevent any person who may be holding the office of President, or acting as President during the term within which this article becomes operative from holding the office of President or acting as President during the remainder of such term.

Section 2.

This article shall be inoperative unless it shall have beenratified as an amendment to the Constitution by the Legislatures of three fourths of the several states within

seven years from the date of its submission to the states by the Congress.

ARTICLE XXI

Section 1.

The right of citizens of the United States of Africa to vote in any primary or other election for President or Vice President, for electors for President or Vice President, or for Senator or Representative in Congress, shall not be denied or abridged by the United States of Africa or any state by reason of failure to pay any poll tax or other tax.

Section 2.

The Congress shall have power to enforce this article by appropriate legislation.

ARTICLE XXII

Section 1.

In case of the removal of the President from office or of his death or resignation, the Vice President shall become President.

Section 2.

Whenever there is a vacancy in the office of Vice President, the President shall nominate a Vice President who shall take office upon confirmation by a majority vote of both Houses of Congress.

Section 3.

Whenever the President transmits to the President pro tempore of the Senate and the Speaker of the House of Representatives his written declaration that he is unable to discharge the powers and duties of his office, and until he transmits to them a written

declaration to the contrary, such powers and duties shall be discharged by the Vice President as acting President.

Section 4.

Whenever the Vice President, and a majority of either the principal officers of the executive departments or of such other body as Congress may by law provide, transmit to the President pro tempore of the Senate and the speaker of the House of Representatives their written declaration that the President is unable to discharge the powers and duties of the office as Acting President.

Thereafter, when the President transmits to the President **pro tempore** of the Senate and the speaker of the House of Representatives his written declaration that no inability exists, he shall resume the powers and duties of his office unless the Vice President and a majority of either the principal officers of the executive department or of such other body as Congress may by law provide, transmit within four days to the President pro tempore of the Senate and the speaker of the House of Representatives their written declaration that the President is unable to discharge the powers and duties of his office. Thereupon Congress shall decide the issue, assembling within forty eight hours for that purpose if not in session. If the Congress, within twenty one day after receipt of the latter written declaration, or if Congress is not in session, within twenty one days after Congress is required to assemble, determined by two third vote of both Houses that the President is unable to discharge the powers and duties of this office, the Vice President shall resume the powers and duties of his office.

ARTICLE XXIII

Section 1.

The right of citizens of the United States of Africa, who are eighteen years of age or older, to vote shall not be denied or abridged by the United States or by any state on account of their age.

ARTICLE XXIV

No law, varying the compensation for the services of the Senators and Representatives, shall take effect, until an election of Representatives shall have interv.

3. The starry golden spiral, the flag, and its meaning.

The United States of Africa flag

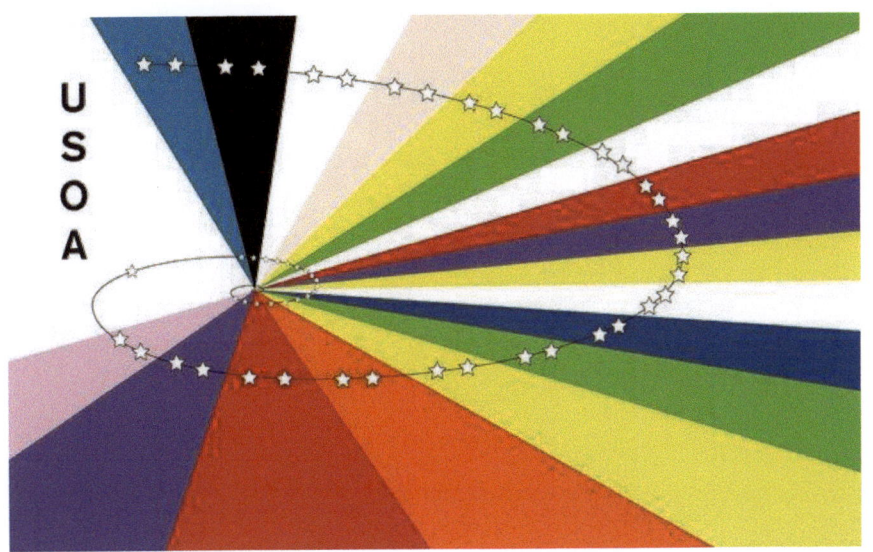

This meaning

The USOA flag is a 10/19 proportioned flag named "Stars on Gold Spiral" or the "starry gold spiral with rainbow colors.

It is composed of 18 bundles with rainbow colors, going from the center to the extremities of the spiral, weaved in three color lines (red, yellow and, blue).

Going from the center, the gold spiral (counter-clockwise) travels through the rainbow. In the middle of each bundle, one can find a five-pointed star (18 stars + 1 outside).

When the gold spiral goes through the rainbow again (one step from the helix), one can find in the middle of each bundle and on the line, two (2) five-pointed stars (36 stars)

The total number is 18 + 36 + 1 which makes 55 stars

The 55 stars represent 54 states of the continent added to 1 (for overseas) united to constitute the United States of Africa, or else the African United States.

The golden spiral has a partial "eadem mutata resurgo" characteristic, which means that is O center remains the same from πet d'angle π/ 2 ; it is thus nearly a logarithmic spiral with m defined by $e_{mπ/2}$ = phi,

a polar equation $\rho = a\varphi^{\frac{\theta}{\pi/2}}$ going through points A, A', A" etc...

Every time it goes round the golden spiral radius is multiplied by $\varphi^4 \simeq 6{,}9$; the tangential polar angle constant value is

$$\psi = \operatorname{arc cot}\left(\frac{2}{\pi}\ln\varphi\right) \simeq 73°$$

The USOA flag shows the divine proportion which result will be in proportion with the law of the universe.

4. The anthem of the Light carriers

Aton Anthem, psalm, this anthem is said to have been written by Amenhotep IV / Akhenaton.

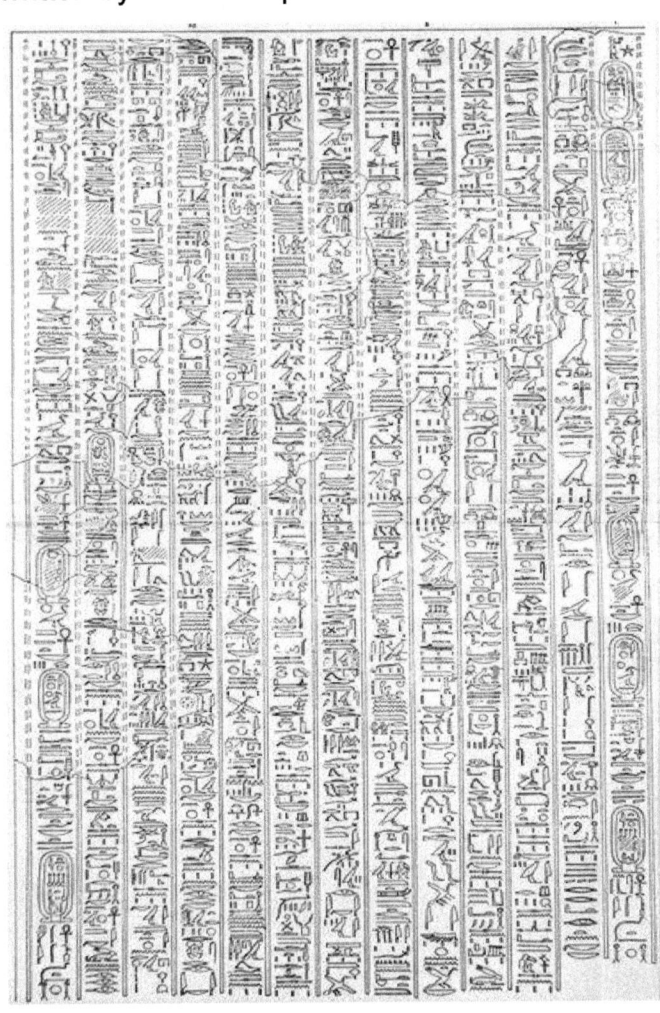

- Line 1 :

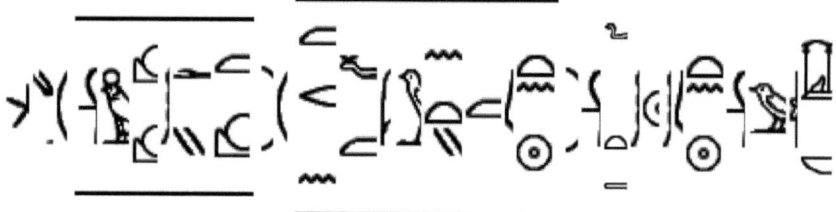

- Line 2 :

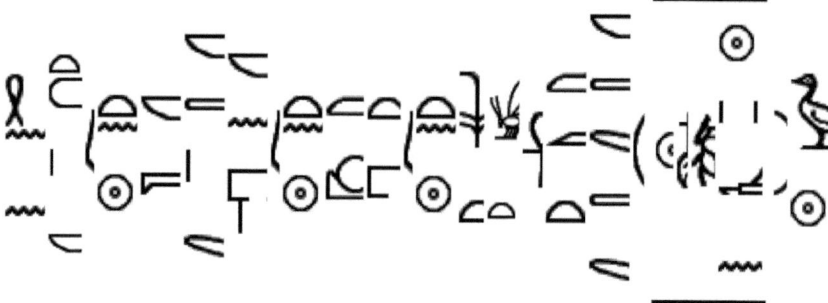

- Line 3 :

- Line 4 :

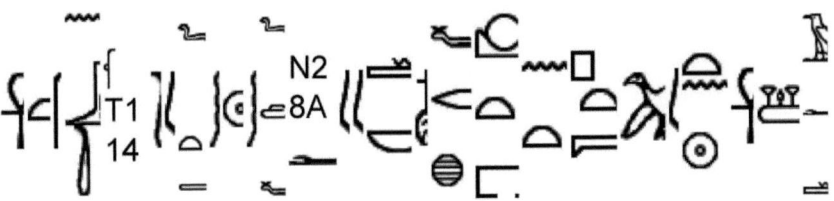

- Line 5 :

- Line 6 :

- Line 7 :

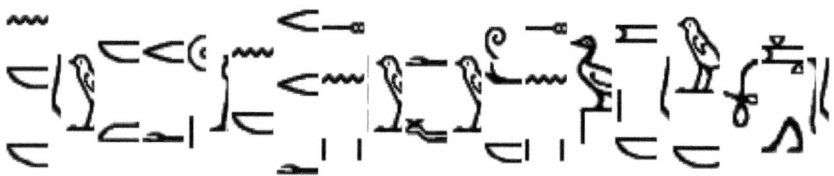

- Line 8 :

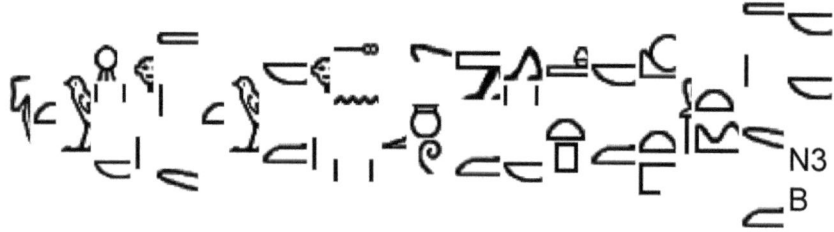

- Line 9 :

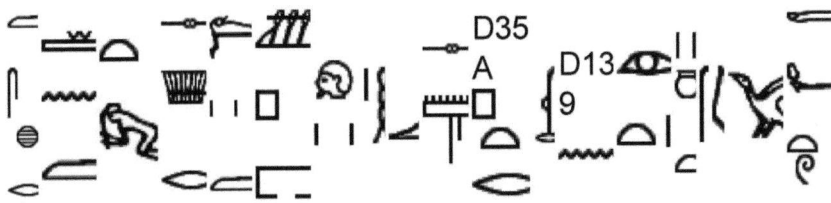

- Line 10 :

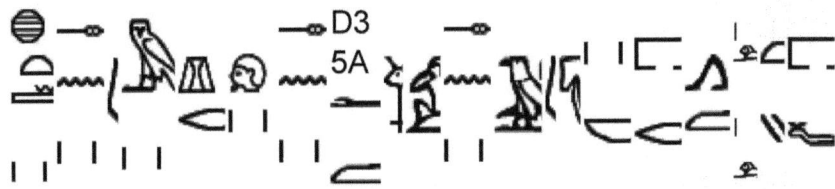

- Line 11 :

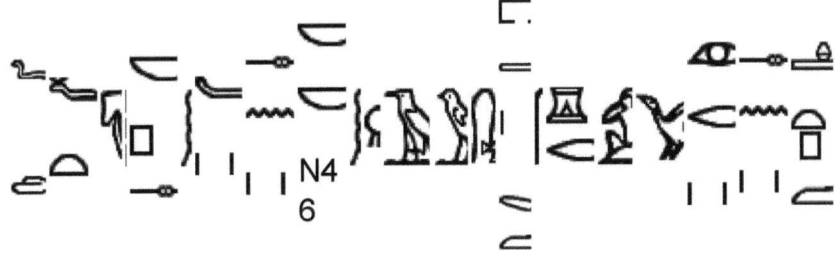

- Line 12 :

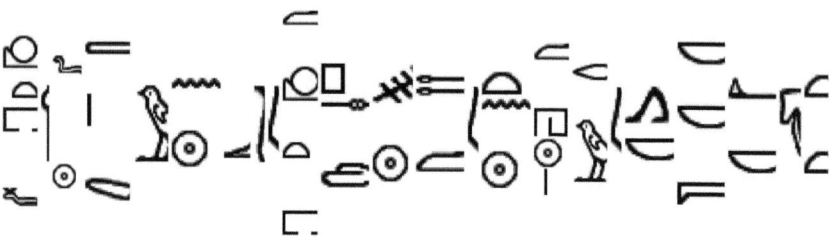

- Line 13 :

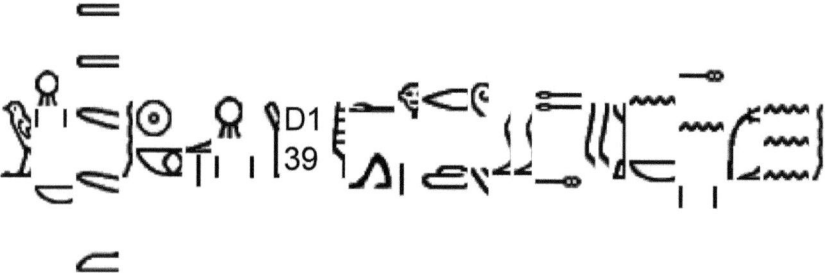

- Line 14 :

USOA Anthem (from Aton Akhenaton)

Hymne des USOA (from the hymn to Aton of Akhenaton)

You rise beautifully in the skyline,

Living Sun, who has been there since the beginning

You shine in the Eastern skyline

Every country is filled with your beauty

You are beautiful, great, bright, you Rise above every country,

All of them being embraced to the outer confines of your universe.

(The audience chants the refrain)

Mmm Mmm Mmm   Mmm Mmm Mmm   Mmm Mmm Mmm Mmm

Eééh éééh éééh   éééh éééh éééh   éééh éééh éééh éééh

Oôô oôôo ôôô   ôôô ôôô ôôô   ôôô ôôô ôôô   ôôô

They have wholly surrendered to you Re,

All of them linked one to another for the sake of your beloved Son.

Although you are far away, your rays get to the earth

You are the men's whole face, we know nothing of your venues.

When you lie in the West, under the skyline,

The earth lies shadowy, as if dead..

At dawn, you shine in the horizon, all enlightened by you, the sun ;

(The audience chants the refrain)

Mmm Mmm Mmm   Mmm Mmm Mmm   Mmm Mmm Mmm Mmm

Eééh éééh éééh   éééh éééh éééh   éééh éééh éééh éééh

Oôô oôôo ôôô   ôôô ôôô ôôô   ôôô ôôô ôôô   ôôô

At daytime, darkness is driven off by your rays.

The fifteen countries wake up lively, men get on their feet,

Thanks to you, they clean up their bodies, put their clothes on;

Open their arms in adoration with your wakening,
The entire earth is at work.

(The audience chants the refrain)

Mmm Mmm Mmm   Mmm Mmm Mmm   Mmm Mmm Mmm
Mmm

Eééh éééh éééh   éééh éééh éééh   éééh éééh éééh
éééh

Oôô oôôo ôôô   ôôô ôôô ôôô   ôôô ôôô ôôô   ôôô

You give spirit to whatever created by you
So mysterious to our eyes are your creations !
Your heart created the earth, although you were all alone,
Putting each man where they belong
With their own different languages,
Special characteristics and skin colors ;
Wherever you can be far away or very near,

(The audience chants the refrain)

Mmm Mmm Mmm   Mmm Mmm Mmm   Mmm Mmm Mmm
Mmm

Eééh éééh éééh   éééh éééh éééh   éééh éééh éééh
éééh

Oôô oôôo ôôô   ôôô ôôô ôôô   ôôô ôôô ôôô   ôôô

Posture of the citizen during the anthem

While singing the hymn, the citizens of the United States of Africa show their attachment to the ideals of their nation by holding their hands and arms open over their heads (as shown on the photo above), and chant during refrains.

Kemetic Sun Salutation is partially done (position 1 et position 11)

Hands are joined and put right before the face, then arms are lifted over the head, with open palms towards the sky, so that the whole body be ready to receive the sublime fragrance.

The 21th century shall be either spiritual or non existent (nuclear destruction). Every morning this chant may be recited prior to the 'Sun salutation' , with the left hand on the heart and the right hand index lifted right in the middle of the forehead.

I am grateful my Lord for the return of my own consciousness.

I am grateful my Lord that you gave me the privilege to participate, one more day to the fulfillment of your plans in order to pursue my own personal change at this stage of comprehension.

Keep me endlessly in touch with your own conscience and grant me the privilege to receive whatever necessary inspiration. Let that be! !

5. The motto, the seal and the crest of this gathered Africa

In God we remain !

Such is the motto of the United States of Africa -USOA lying on the mâât foundation, reminded to us by the scribe COOVI RECHMIRE; (relevance, truth, righteousness, transparency, equity, rectitude, welfare, solidarity, sharing).

To believe or not in God is not relevant as far as "melanized" people are concerned for they carry the light when it comes to their enormous storage capacity and daylight synthesis.

They are searching how to express and how to show the divinity inside the density of the material.

A participative quest, through the physical body (in its mortal condition), musically stirred by cosmic harmony. We remain in and with Him.

Just a sparkle of His divine conscience arrived to admire the work, the garden of splendors, the manifested universe made visible to our eyes by the daylight star.

That is how God made everything, in a divine proportion (gold number)

This has already been integrated in his residual memory so that he sees to it that :

- they will not stoop to the level of beast (cruelty), though he usually react the same way animals' body do.

- mating with animals is a totally forbidden transgression.

There can be no archetypal hybridization thanks to natural selection.

- they will not destroy their habitation (the earth) due to an insatiable hunger for earthy goods.

The emptiness is surrounded by cosmic harmony which maintains the balance of the universe.

- they will not put an end to the species diversity.

- they will not forget that men are sun worshippers, the very source of life.

The seal of Union; the solar seal

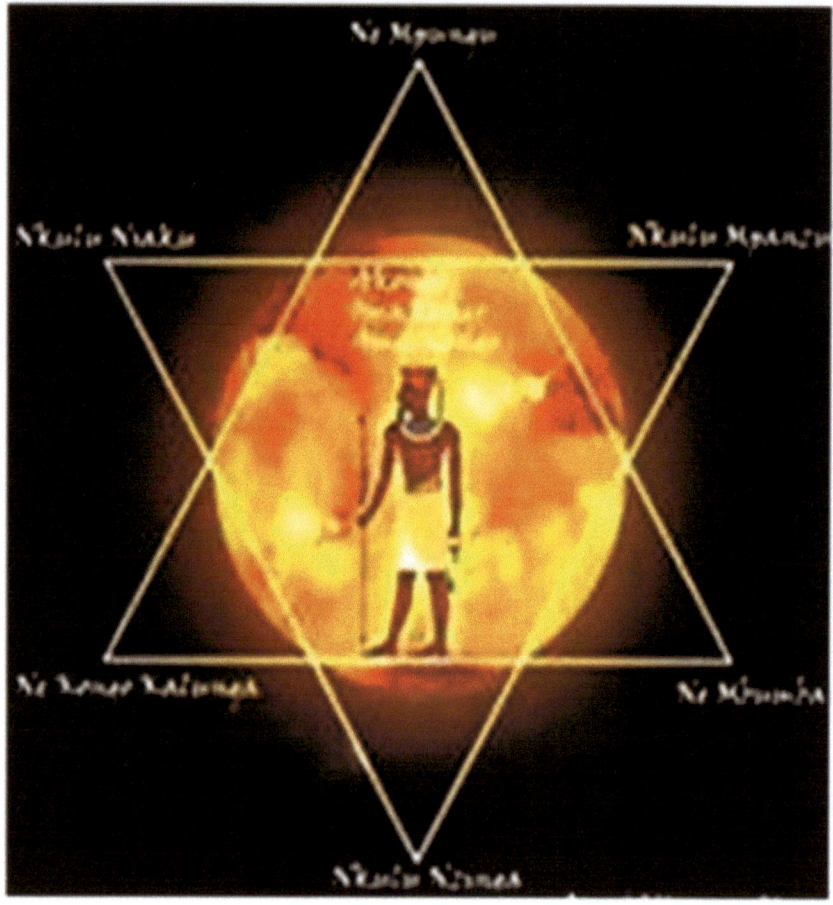

Kalunga

The Union Crest

The eye of Horus, the eye of God who sees everything and from whom everything emanates in a golden progressive order

MaatMatatu!

God made everything in proportion and gave it vibration with a numeric correspondence, in a hierarchical order in beings and things.

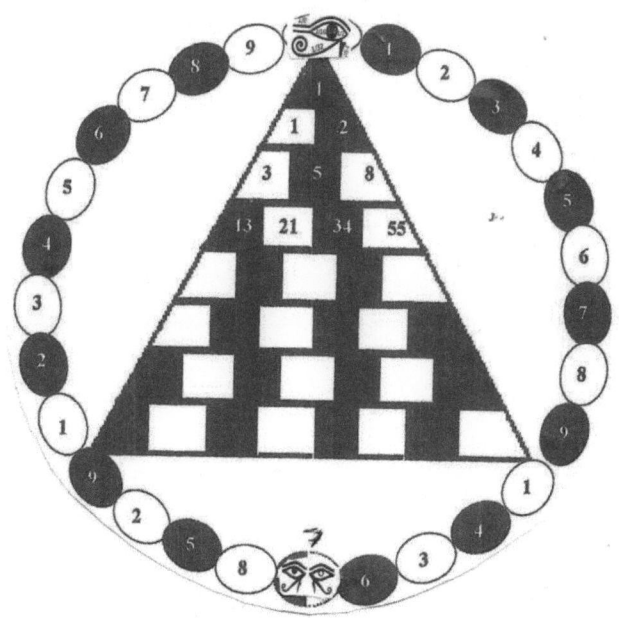

Kongéla !

Gather whatever is fractured and scattered away.

6. PanAfrican emergencies

September 14, 2019 challenge against the agreement of ECO currency to the euro, which result ipso facto to the extension of the CFA zone to the other African countries is absolutely legitimate, because the euro is a far too strong

Currency for the economy of African countries. The fake stability of fixed parity will only destroy their growth. Although having been set free the former slaves do not wish to leave the original comfort, of the farm, they will rather choose to be paid for their work. The slave owners are working on it.

The second emergency challenge is to say NO TO NUCLEAR plants in Africa. The energy potential (hydroelectricity, wind, sun, sea et gas) is so GIGANTIC, that Africa has

no need whatsoever to import the nuclear danger at so high a cost. The ultimate goal of these nuclear plants that are proposed to some African countries is to have a place to store China and Russia nuclear wastes.

De-forestation and the selling of our lands are real emergency challenges that should mobilize our citizens to be organized wildly in Africa against that.

Anticipation

Black people remain way too emotional when it comes to implement this challenge.

They need to think "coldly" and anticipate in how to make a long term strategy real. African and Pan African people ambitions and ideals must be firmly defined. Kemi Seba can lead the way and be our powerful voice.

The echo of the clamoring ECO bell, in Africanists collective unconsciousness, is to put an end to existing micro-states and kinglets for good.

Anticipation 1: Symbolic creation of the United States of Africa

UNITED STATES OF AFRICA

Produce a comprehensive report of the texts (constitution) and all symbols related to the federal state (flag, coat of arms, etc.) which will be symbolic declaration of the birth of USOA and inauguration of the moral authority that shall represent the nation wherever needed.

This moral authority (the pointed end of the spear) will be the first political embryo, that will lead to the effective existence of the United States of Africa. There will be initiatives taken, while keeping up with the latest news stories, for ourselves (Africans and people from African descent), shaking us up from the slavery torpor to action and then to anticipation.

A USOA box (containing a flag, sheets and, badge) will be sent to every citizen/political party/ association and government.

The content will be spelled out and issued online on www.usoafrica.org and www.usoaditunga.org for free.

The incoming generations must be formatted, and ready for the creation of an African federal state.

Anticipation 2 : Creation of African gold reserves

Nobody would think of a federal state that would not have its currency (EU, USA, Russia, Brazil, China, India)

Private owners are going to create the gold and currency reserves of the continent. They will benefit from a special permit agreed by the government with the support of a sitting president (that of Ghana for example). This same bank will also act as a Caisse des Dépôts et Consignations to further debt for all African countries.

This private business buys the gold produced everywhere in Africa (under pan African agreement signed by producing countries) at a preferential price.

Gold reserves will be progressively constituted, and plans are to get the same level of gold and currency reserves than that of the USA Federal Reserves.

How?

The powerful voice of Kemi will be heard everywhere in Africa so everyone will contribute one dollar a day. PanAfricanists will contribute until it reaches an amount of 360 dollars a year for 500millions of inhabitants. All of them will become small shareholders.

Subscriptions will be received through mobile money accounts that can be open in every country.

Not to mention wealthy countries or people all over the world who want to invest their money somewhere.

All the African states producing gold will be invited to sell their gold at a special price to the African Gold Reserves Cash. That will be expressing positive sovereignty.

The gold reserves bank will then become the incubator of USOA single currency thanks to its reserves which will enable it to fix the reference rate with the agreement of secondary central banks.

Anticipation 3. Dissemination of Knowledge in African languages

VOCALIZING all the knowledge accumulated by humanity in order to make it available to every African in every spoken language throughout Africa, starting with wolof language.

With the new technologies and learning modes, the oral method which is widely spread and used in Africa will facilitate the acquisition of knowledge for the African people.

Facilitate the access of academic knowledge to the greater number of young people, through oral books, oral lessons in schools and universities throughout Senegal and ultimately West Africa.

Provide free access to talking books through the platform, by using a smartphone application and the internet. Widely spread the use of oral/spoken text books (lessons and exercises included), with programs implemented by the ministry of National Education for every country concerned, for primary, secondary and university level.

Provide every library of every school with paper books so that parents will not have to make anymore expense for academic books.

Prepare the education of an academic elite, a qualified workforce in order for them to be ready and available whenever companies need of them due to the induced economic upturn; in conformity with sustainable development goals.

Anticipation 4 and 5. Fresh water and arable Lands resources

Produce and carry fresh water throughout the continent towards dried lands, after desalination.

Why do we sell our arable lands to the Chinese or anyone else? Kemi Seba powerful voice is once again going to be raised and tell everything about these enormous deals taking place in each and every country.

Anticipation 6

Abundant production of electricity with locally refined minerals.

Locally refined minerals have two major benefits :

1. local extraction and transformation reduce environmental impact
2. better production costs

Anticipation 7

A desirable future for humanity added to a good strategy as regards this future.

When it comes to build up Africa, we African people (kamites) are talking about the desirable future of Humanity on the whole.

The good strategy is to associate our human brothers, the indo-europeans (white people actually) for three reasons ;

- there is only one human race ethnically divided in three

 main groups (black, white and yellow)

- facilitate the integration of white people in a black continent in order to teach them what universal brotherhood is about without their being obsessed by total domination

And work together for a better comprehension of the scales values for the protection of our commonly shared habitacle; the earth.

- No one is going to a B planet, after having destroyed our earth. The people who favour the rise of "aryans" are surely working for their own domination, but the natural selection rate taking place in the hybrids remains static (25 %).

- The great replacement has no chance to take place (Noah's arch for the preservation of all kind of species) all our energy must be focused on creating instead of contesting about easily solved problems. May God help to us to be not only outstanding warriors (enduring, persevering and resilient), but open to listen and understand things the right way in order to build new Humanity.

Yôga Yôga Yôga (listen, liste, listen)

Azambé, â Zambé, Azambé (God and his numerous manifestations)

Ngui lè mbé, (so I talked, so I said, say the 'akoua' from northern Congo B)

7. Backbone and foundations of the federal state

The pillars and foundations are :

They are the political and citizens who will create :

- The constitution, the flag and the motto of the federal state USOA by the civil society, shall symbolize the way to alleviate things.

Economic sovereignty

- The Golden Reserves Office of Deposits and Consignation
- MOSSOLO, single currency, with the support of the Gold federal reserves

Cultural independence(getting away from the chains of mental slavery)

- Matatu, the search engine, with African culture content
- building a replica of the Saqqara pyramid (same size than the ooriginal), in the moutains between Sequoue and

Parakou ; a special place for a rise at spiritual and scientific level.

- building smaller replicas of Saqqara pyramid in each state member of the Union in order for them to become connecting places at spiritual and scientific level.

The vision

The building of the desirable future of humanity, Africa.

The building of this Africa will be real

- In bringing fresh water to arid lands inside the continent, following desalination, so as to quantify, what needed vegetables and fruit trees are to be planted in order to provide food security and support the citizens purchase power.

- Promoting ecology through recycling ; exhaustive waste recycling and enhancing metal recycling and re-using due to the coming rarefaction of metals, cleaning of oceans, rivers and cities.

- Maintaining group forests systems, through massive reforestation

   Wood operation on reforested spaces;

- Being extremely wary before the nuclear danger despite the energy potential;

- Local transformation of minerals ; thus limiting the environmental impact and lower production costs of materials derived from minerals extracted on our continent;

- Make sure that our continent remains a melting-pot for all ethnical groups (black, white, yellow) as there is only one human race, despite the color differences due to melanin.

Next Chronogramme

2020: Creation, symbolic and solemn, of the federal state, USOA.

Establishment, on an interim basis, of federal institutions.

2020: private plan to build up gold reserves, from Africa

2021: private search engine with African content

8. Action taken to build the desirable future for Humanity

With all the mining resources, the amazing energetic potential and the strong young demography of the continent, are the African people able to build this desirable future for Humanity ? Once the federal state has financed the FRESH WATER Project « production and transportation of fresh water to the arid lands situated inside Africa, right after desalination of sea water», each citizen will be guaranteed at least the minimum of a purchase power.

Food security will not depend anymore on imports, nor emergency aid or whether hazards, because the presence of water in these arid lands will ensure an all year long agricultural production instead of 2 months a year.

The entire production of gold within the continent has to be bought in order to constitute the USOA federal state gold reserve, the objective being to gather 10 thousand tons of gold.

The geographical distribution of the USOA bodies and works headquarter.

- the gold reserves and the deposit and consignation Office at ACCRA ;

- The Senate at ABUJA
- The House of Representatives at Ouagadougou
- The federal capital city at Freetown (Sierra Leone)
- The pyramid of Saqqara's replica in Benin

Appendix

1. Press Release
2. The Gold Reserve of Africa Bank, through a call to encourage savings
3. The African Fresh Water Project
4. The search engine with an African content
5. The tremendous potential for energy
6. On-site refining of African minerals
7. The 50,000 km railway system to be built
8. The Gas Terminal Project at Kaolack, Senegal
9. The Gas Terminal of Pointe-Noire, Congo
10. The University Centres
11. The Congo River Festival
12. The contribution of the aviation industry to the integration of the continent
13. The KRUMAH Plan for Africa: the foundation of the African Federal State

1. Press Release

We are pleased to inform the public that belongs to the USOA area of the

CIVIL SOCIETY AND CITIZENS MEETING
To be held at Accra, Cotonou, Abuja, Kinshasa
In the current 2020 year

Topic of the 2020 session

Relevance as regards the launching of a Federal State in Africa

Day 0: Participants Welcoming
        Debates, Validation, and Adoption of the constitution project
Day 1: Debates and approval of emblem; flag, hymn, currency, the capital city
        Debates and approval of the "backbones and foundation of the Federal State
Day 2: Solemn Ceremony for the symbolic birth of the United States of Africa (USOA)
        Election of the temporary leaders

Detailed information on the event will be available
Observations and written contribution may be sent to www.usoa.org or mailed to usoa@gmail.com
Phone number :
Postal address P.O. Box :

Press Release

We are informing the community in faith and the public of the organization of the

MEETING OF THE IMAMS OF THE USOA AREA

N'Djamena (TCHAD)

Courant 2020

From 12th to 14th May, 2020

Theme topic of the 2020 session

Peace through Islam in the USOA area

Day 1 : Reception of Imams and Believers,

Debates, validation and adoption of the project agreement with the BOKO HARAM Believers

Day 2 : Debates and approbation ;

Speaking time of Boko Haram delegates before the rest of Believers

Dialogue between Believers for a religion of peace

Day 3 : Solemn ceremony of the symbolic birth of PEACEFUL ISLAM within the USOA

Election of the three interim executive leaders

Detailed information about this event will be

Made available

Comments and contributions should be sent to

www.usoa.org and mailed to : usoa@gmail.com

phone :

Mailing Address P.O. Box

2. The Gold Reserve of Africa Bank, through a call to encourage savings

The entire gold production will be bought to make USOA Federal State gold reserve, the aim being to get to the amount of ten thousand (10,000) tons of gold per site, which makes a total 50.000 tons a year.

DEMONSTRATION OF THE INTEREST AND CALL FOR PRIVATE AND PUBLIC SAVINGS

I.   Strategic targeted point

To get to the "backbones and foundations" of the United States of Africa (following the Civil Society and African NGO's Days), Ghana is launching this call to public and private saving to collect its share (10,000 tons). Through this, every citizen will participle in the mobilization of necessary funds to implement the Gold Reserve of Africa, one of the backbones and foundations" of the African Federal State (UAS-USOA).

II.   Issues and Challenges

a. The priority of challenge concerned: the constitution of the gold reserve

The absolute priority of the USOA federal state, following its symbolic proclamation, is the constitution of the Africa Gold reserve, which obtains 10 thousand tons of gold per site within 10 years which will amount to 50,000 tons for 5 sites.

III. The total amount of the action taken per citizen citizen

This emphasized call for public and private saving exhort every citizen to take action by saving one (01) dollar a day, bank holidays included, during ten (10) years.

This is to be done through mobile money accounts and selected agencies in which location in Africa will be given.

IV. Total Amount of action for companies and financial institutions

A yearly 500 US dollar fixed share for a total of 100 million shares for 10 years. The shares will be remunerated at 5% which will be allocated every 15th of January starting from year +1.

V. Useful information as regard subscriptions

ITEMS	Details
Gold Reserve to be **constituted**	50,000 tons within 10 years, whereas 5,000 a year
Buying cost at the actual rate of 45,000 euros per kg	2 250 000 000 000 withing 10 years which make 225 000 000 000 euros a year

The total amount of money subscription	2 250 billion euros in 10 years, which make 225 billion euros a year which make 0,616 5 billion euros, which makes 616,5 million euros a day
One-half of the shares kept for citizens	300 million a day subscribed, for a minimum of (01) euro per citizen
The other half for companies and the financial market	316 million euros a day, subscribed with a minimum of 500 euros with no maximum limit with a per capita availability of shares
Duration and validity period	10 years starting July 2020
Interest Rate	5% payable on January 15th of year + 1

VI. Subscription and payment through mobile money

For the forthcoming ten years small shareholders (less than 360 euros), subscription and payment of interest will be made through mobile money, by recording id's and photos, JPEG scanning (photos), and sent to designated local banks, with no additional fees.

The operations will be validated when further information and additional data will be completed.

VII.   Conditions of projects' implementation reception closing date

In addition to the usual facilitation of the investment code, this project will benefit from total exoneration for the five following years, for all equipment and material needed. The proposals related to financing and partnership will be sent immediately to the pilot bank headquarter, the Bank of Ghana.

Done at (ACCRA) (COTONOU) (ABUJA) (KINSHASA)

On...
....

The President

3. The African Fresh Water Project

Manifestation of interest

Call for contribution and projects

I.   **Targeted sustainable development and strategic objective**

A search for partners for the implementation of the above-listed projects to make the challenge of sustained development and emergence real.

II. **Prioritized challenges**

N° 1 Challenge or priority

The absolute challenge for Africa is the following:

The production of freshwater, by using seawater desalination, and transportation throughout Africa arid lands, especially into the Sahelian zone will be the main project (an emergency and a priority) that will benefit the African continent.

Central Africa

- Beginning from Kribi, Lake Chad, and Ngaoundere (South Sudan), a water lining, situated next to the pipeline network carrying oil from Doha to Kribi. Lake Chad may be gradually replenished daily, up to its original level.
  The arid lands will be made cultivable from the south Chad area to North Cameroon, as well as Central

Africa, so that fruits and vegetables may grow thanks to the presence of freshwater.

- from Lobito to the arid lands in the southern area of Angola.

West Africa

- From Nouhadibou to Kidal, Timbuktu and Agadez
- From Nouakchott to Mopti, the river Niger will be gradually supplied with fresh water, daily
- From Saint Louis to Kayes, Senegal river will be gradually supplied with fresh water, daily
- From Kaolack to Kedougou/Saraya, also to cultivate the lands within Senegal
- From Ziguinchor (to have cultivable land throughout Casamance area), in Sikasso Joliba river will be gradually supplied with fresh water daily
- From San Pedro to Bobo Dioulasso, the lands in the northern area of Ivory Coast and south Burkina Faso (from Tabu to Taï, Samatiguila, Manankoro, from Grand Lahou to Daloa, Korhogo, Ouangolodugu all the arid lands will be watered down.
- From Newtown to Kotuba, Gaua, and Ouagadougou
- From Cotonou to Malanville, Tillabery to Aagades land in the area od south Niger will be watered. The Niger river will be gradually supplied with fresh water daily at Tillabery.
- Bypasses at Sokoto – Dosso – Niamey – Dosso - Zinder-Diffa -Sokoto-Kitsna- Maiduguri- Lake Chad

will pinpoint Nigeria in the project, from Bodogri, Shaki, Kalomo, Koko, Tambawell, Sokoto.

East Africa

- From Djibouti (and Somali land)in Ethiopia and Erythrea to Sudan, the entire lands will be cultivable in the easter part of Africa where famine and drought usually reign.
- From Mombasa to the northern area of Kenya, South Sudan
- From Maputo to Matebele Land the drylands of Zimbabwe will be watered

Egypt

- From Alexandria to the southern border of the desert zone, the drylands will be watered gradually, while the Nile river will be gradually supplied with fresh water.

Lybia

- From Benghazi to the Lybian desert zone, the Tubu lands from Chad up to the end of Agades (Niger).

Southern Africa

- From Walis Bey to Malawi lands, from Botswana to Kalahari desert
- From Durban to Lesotho arid lands and the northern area of South Africa

Madagascar

- From Toamasina to Ambrositra
- Mananjary to IHOSY
- Androka to BFTSIOKY
- TSARATANANA to North East (BEFANDRIANA)

A long-term (50 years) indebtedness to alleviate the consequences of the fresh waterway and reduce poverty by increasing the irrigated perimeters and in doing so, improve the fruit and vegetable output. Selling freshwater will enable reimburse the loan thanks to a private management company.

One project to free Africa from famine, poverty, from massive import of subsistence food and long-term aid.

Project

Erythrea Fresh Water
EFW

Erythrea Fresh Water, the visible part of Africa basic need. One project to free the whole continent from severe hardship. EFW program wants to implement production and transportation of fresh water through the hinterland arid lands following a great deal of sea desalinization, that is to sayone million m^3a day.

Statements

With a young population (60%), Africa remains a promising continent, and the desirable future for humanity.

In view of meeting challenges such as, combating poverty, the development of living standards, facilitating access to water with a good quality drinking water and a political will to let Erythrea become an emerging country in 2025, this project is initialized by the state : Erythrea Fresh Water - EFW.

It is obviously a matter of :
- Ensuring availability of fresh water throughout the territory
- Making water clean and safe for the country including cities and villages
- Bringing fresh water within entire Erythrea so as to significantly increase irrigated areas,
- Planting abundantly fruit trees and vegetables in the country
- Facilitating and enhancing the implementation of food industry
- Harmonization and standardization of Erythrea agriculture production at a high quality level

The lack of fresh drinking water in the immense area including Erythrea, Ethiopia, Sudan, means the perpetuation of famine factor, poverty and underdevelopment, while in the same time being a challenge to be met and positively solved.

The Erythrean state plans to implement the PRODUCTION AND TRANSPORTATION OF FRESH WATER THROUGHOUT THE TERRITORY BY WAY OF SEA DESALINIZATION.

Problems to be solved

Consequently Erythrea, is willing as a coastal country, to improve its organization and management, in order to enhance its own production and distribution of fresh water within the country and even in Ethiopia.

> The installation of five desalinization units with a daily capacity of 200 000 m^3, equivalent to a capacity of one million de m^3 per site for a total of two sites ; Tiyo and another yet to be chosen.

> The installation of transportation infrastructures (pipe-line and territory networking), storage (water towers and tanks) for villages and agriculture areas, small and middle size potable water units, tailored to the needs of each agglomeration.

> The creation of the private company for the management of production and transportation of fresh water (ERYTHREA WATERS), with the detention of 30 per cent of the capital by the state of Erythrea

> The anticipated signature of the WATER PURCHASE AGREEMENT under the supervision of the government of Erythrea, between ERYTHREA WATERS (a steering committee will be set up), existing and future distribution companies, local communities and stakeholders banks ensuring funding arrangements for the selling of water to wholesale distributors.

> Generate a policy for fruit trees and vegetables planting on irrigated lands, loaned to private farmers might they be local or foreigners, (from one to five hectares) and for industrial operation on larger lands (up to 10 hectares).

> Initialize a policy of technical and financial assistance for nationals in the creation of fruit and vegetable-based food industries.

> Training people in technical, management and leadership areas. Technical and financial training to invest in purchasing equipment and early learning materials, fruit and vegetable production, according to new environmental standards.

> Most of the farm staff (our farmers will) has been trained on-the-job and doesn't have the necessary experience or qualification for their jobs (traditional knowledge has not dispensed to new generation).

'Sunugal&Africa' Digest, written and formated, with each NAICCE & MATICIA project, according to RSE methods and tools– Free Document

106

Potential beneficiaries and expected results

Beneficiaries targeted :

- The government of Senegal has been assigned by the Head of State to aim its efforts at promoting effective poverty reduction of the Senegalese citizen by facilitating access to drinking water through;
- Water distribution companies (existing and future ones) through the liberalization of water distribution sector, including in the remotest villages of the country
- Local committees and regional councils by increasing the number of areas irrigated by existing fresh water
- Those living along the Senegal river, through their activities 'agriculture and aquaculture operations'
- Senegalese people by enabling access to drinking water, thanks to its availability, throughout the country
- Senegalese social and economic actors (service providers) who will benefit from all necessary good-quality water (plenty of water supply on time within the country) critical to their operations.

Expected Results:

1. Long term results :

Permanent availability of fresh water, all over the country.
Build all the necessary infrastructures related to the production and transportation of fresh water, after sea water desalinization operated on three sites
Revegetate the arythrean desert with fruit trees
Make aquaculture industry possible by injecting small doses of fresh water on a daily basis, in the blue Nile river,
The sale of fresh water to the neighbouring countries (Ethiopia, Sudan), will provide them with the necessary amount of currency
A sustainable financing (a 25/30 years loan) that will be reimbursed thanks to the sale of water
Extend the project to Egypt

2. Middle-term results :

The state will be equipped with a tool to solve the national and difficult problem of supplying the country with fresh and drinkable water
The state will have a powerful tool to reduce efficiently the poverty level and allow the country to become emergent

With this project the following results will be obtained:

- Diagnose the real needs in fresh and drinking water of the country;
- Identify the existing infrastructures, access, production capacities, the collection of the useful information, about what type of infrastructures are needed to achieve the defined objective;
- Develop criteria for eligibility of the sites of desalinization, to see which network layout must be chosen for the storage works;
- Determine the costs of the system and financial engineering as well as expand the on-site logistics;
- Support the development of the management project.

'Sunugal&Africa' Digest, written and formated, with each NAICCE & MATICIA project, according to RSE methods and tools- Free Document

THE PROPOSED RESPONSIBLE SOLUTION

The lenghty stoppage in water supplies in urban cities, lack of water in the countryside and the increase in needs due to the rapid development growth and human activities are a severe impediment the development of the country.
Water shortage in the Sahelo-Sahelian area remain the main cause for poverty, famine and conflicts
The study is done in order to examine the feasability to implement infrastructures of WATER PRODUCTIONAND TRANSPORTATION THROUGHOUT ERYTHREA, BY SEA WATER DESALINIZATION
The study will highlight the opportunities offered by the increase of irrigated lands, water consumption and transportation
The study will allow to give an enlightened opinion on quality control laboratory, and potential agrobusiness industries.
The legal issue will be anticipated to "ERYTHREAN WATERS", tin view to secure the reimbursement of the loan.

1. 4. BENEFICIARIES ET ACTORS

- The Government endowed to implement this project in order to increase production, transportation and distribution of fresh water throughout the country
- The farmers and all the industry need to increase the number of qualified staffin order to get better results
- In order to support this project, the state will be intentional about building capacity of all the persons with management duties and available staff in activities related to production, le transportation and distribution of fresh water ;
- The service providers will be supervised, in order to work in conformity to the referential rules according to the international standards.

The Project guidance :7

The state approach being based on deficiencies and the necessity to get to development, the Project will be managed by a designated expert from NAICCE and MATICIA, with the help of the concerned ministry officials.

Cost, duration and financing program of the Project studies:

The six-months cost estimation of the Project to be implemented is one million euros, with two expected workshops, the first one to validate the mid-term report, and a subregional workshop to validate the final report of the project.

THE SUSTAINABLE OPPORTUNITY

This project is a sustainable answer to the need of the population for fresh drinking water, with the opportunity given by bringing fresh water to the arid landsinside Africa.

The point is to validate the production of plenty of fresh water, thanks to the sea water desalinization at a basic cost of 100 FCFA per m3.

The economic impact of the projection Africa.

The implementation of production, transportation and distribution of fresh water throughout the country will allow the different actors of the agricultural sector to offer a high quality production at very competitive price
The availability of fresh drinking water is going to improve deeply the level of health of the populations and support income generating activities.

By doing so, the authorities will permanently be able to maintain the skills required according to international standards in order to ensure food safety, and rebuild a climate of confidence among populations, who are the ones enjoying fresh drinking water.

The production/transportation and distribution of fresh drinking water is the perfect social and economic integration tool in Africa

TECHNOLOGICAL DIVIDE and COMPETITIVE POSITION

It is not necessary to make a review of the technical characteristics and acompetitive performance indicator of technological maturity, for all the equipment and material are already in the public domain and have already been a well-provenseller for years (Israël, Morocco)

There still is no or limited competition considering the investment, the nature of the work to be done, the volume to be produced (transportation and delivery) on remote sites.

ASSETS, DATES 1, KEY FIGURES

April Mayand June July to December 2019	1. Transmission of letter of intent of the Project . 2. Preparation of documents: Project Introduction Document, Business Plan, Booklet with the list of the various jobs, etc. 3. Financing Engineering, with the accounting, legal, patrimonial and fiscal condition 4. Research of financial partners for fundraising
2020 2021 2022	9. Construction starting date: construction of sea water desalinization and installation of new pipes 10.Economic development according to identified level of growth qualified by these new clients 11. Project Launch Phase II and phase III

The estimated global cost of the project at the time of the launch is 875 billions CFA

The management EFW project is a Limited Liability Company, with a registered capital of 50million Cfa (Eur 75000), valued on accounting and patrimonial condition to EUR 200 000, with 100 % retained by the funding members and primary business partners.
The social share is worth EUR 30

MARKET SEGMENTS

The market of supplies offered by EFW presents a number of opportunities as regards:
- a quasi-state monopoly of fresh water producers
- a political will to ensure and increase the level and quality of fresh water in order to meet the increasing need of the populations.
- a high profitability whatever price targeted services are sold and regardless of the financial gains (the law of averages) on the market.
- the sustainable loan proposed in a average of 30 et 50 years.

Except for Erythrea, the project starting point, all the East African countries (Sudan, Ethiopia, Egypt) are potentiallyliable for the development of similar activities

'Sunugal&Africa' Digest. written and formated. with each NAICCE & MATICIA project. according to RSE methods and tools- Free Document

109

STATES & GOVERNMENT + NGO'S
LOCAL TERRITORIAL COLLECTIVITY
NATIONAL COMPANY OF DISTRIBUTION AND NEW PRIVATE OPERATORS
SENEGAL AND NIGER RIVERS SUPERVISORS
PRIVATE LANDOWNERS

The means needed to implement the targeted objectives are crucially improved when the above 5 identified and qualified segments of the market are mastered.

KEY FIGURES OF SIMPLIFIED PROVISIONAL OPERATION

Account Statement in Cfa francs

Loan: 875

Loan Duration: 30 years

Wage rate: 6 %

Annuity

Annual output: 365 000 000 m3

The unit price of m3: 100 Cfa franc

Annual income: 36,5

Items	Annual Amount (Cfa billion)	Annual Totals
Total expenses (loan reimbursement including running costs)	31,5 30 1,5	31,5
Total income	36,5	36,5
Margin	5	5

Figures on 30 years

	Item	Annual Amount (Cfa Billions)	Totals on 30 years (Cfa billions)
Expenses	Loan reimbursement	30	900
	Running costs	1,5	45
	Total expenses	31,5	945
Income	Total income	36,5	1095
Margin	Gross Margin	5	110

AN ECO-FRIENDLY STRUCTURE

Desalinization plants will be solar powered without any hydrocarbon products released into the sea.

CONTACTS

NINEA Number : 007232812   RCCM : SN.DKR.2019.A.

Villa 9967 ZONE A GRAND DAKAR BEHIND EL MANSOUR

FIX : (+221) 33 824 38 87

MOB : (+221) 76 358 08 26 & (+242) 06 452 40 04

Sunugal & Africa Digest	RESPONSIBLE INVESTMENT OPPORTUNITY

Sunugal & Africa Digest n 03-b dated 22/05/2019

Project

Central Africa Fresh Water CAFW

Central Africa FRESH WATER, is the visible part of Africa's basic need. One single project, that will set the continent free from misery and poverty. CAFW is meant to supply the continent with fresh water up to the hinterland arid lands, following a great amount of sea water desalination, about one million m3 every day.

Facts

Because 60 % of its population is young, the African continent remains the place to be and really is the "desirable future" for humanity.

This Central Africa Fresh Water project (CFAW) is being initialized by the States of Central Africa Economic Community (CAEC) in order to fight against poverty, improve people's living standards, facilitate their access to quality water. The objective being to let Africa become the continent of the future.

It is obviously about :
- Ensuring fresh water availability throughout CAEC countries
- Making water clean and safe for the countries including cities and villages
- Bringing fresh water to arid lands situated far inside the countries, in North Cameroon, Chad, North RC and South Sudan, Senegal to significantly increase irrigated areas
- Planting abundantly fruit trees and vegetables in the country ;
- Facilitating and enhancing the implementation of food industry;
- Harmonization and standardization at a high quality level, agricultural production of CAEC countries, especially in the arid areas.

Sunugal & Africa' Digest, written and formatted, for each project, for NAICCE & MATICIA, according to RSE tools and methods -   Free Document

1

The lack of fresh drinking water in the immense semi desert zone of the area CAEC means the perpetuation of famine, poverty and under development, while being perceived a challenge to be met and solved for the greatest benefit of all of us.

CAEC plans to implement PRODUCTION AND TRANSPORTATION OF FRESH WATER THROUGHOUT THE COMMUNITY ARID LANDS BY WAY OF SEA DESALINIZATION
The CAEC littoral being an asset (from Douala to Lobito), it will enable it to improve its organization and management capacities and consequently, enhance production and distribution of fresh water in the targeted arid lands like North Cameroon, Chad, Northern part of Central Africa, South Soudan and South Angola

Problems to be solved

> The installation of five desalinization units with a daily capacity of 200 000 m³, equivalent to a capacity of one (1) million de m³ per site, for two sites ; Kribi, Lobito.
>
> The installation of transportation infrastructures (pipe-lines and territory networking), storage (water towers and tanks) for villages and agricultural areas, small and middle size potable water units, tailored to the needs of each agglomeration
>
> The creation of the private company for the management of production and transportation of fresh water (CENTRAL AFRICA FRESH WATER), with 30 % of the capital, held by the states.
>
> The anticipated signature of the WATER PURCHASE AGREEMENT under the supervision of CAEC and concerned governments between CENTRAL AFRICA FRESH WATERS (a steering committee will be set up), existing and future distribution companies, local communities and stakeholder banks ensuring all the banking arrangements for the selling of water to wholesale distributors.

Problèmes à résoudre

> Generate a policy for fruit trees and vegetable planting on irrigated lands, loaned to private farmers might they be local or foreigners, (from one to five hectares) and for industrial operation on larger lands (up to 10 hectares).
>
> Initialize a policy of technical and financial assistance for nationals in the creation of fruit and vegetable-based food industries.
>
> Training people in technical, management and leadership fields. Technical and financial training to invest in purchasing equipment and early learning materials, fruit and vegetable production, according to new environmental standards.
>
> Most of the farm staff (our farmers will) has been trained on-the-job and do not have the necessary experience or qualification for their jobs (traditional knowledge has not dispensed to new generation).

Senegal & Africa' Digest, written and formatted, for each project, for NAICCE & MATICIA, according to RSE tools and methods -   Free Document

2

Potential beneficiaries and expected results

Targeted beneficiaries :

- Governments, in order to promote the reduction of poverty of the citizen by facilitating access to drinking water through ;
- Water distribution companies (existing and future ones) through the liberalization of water distribution sector, including in the remotest villages of the country
- Local committees and regional councils by increasing the number of areas irrigated by existing fresh water
- Those living along the Chad river, through their activities 'agriculture and aquaculture operations'
- Senegalese people by enabling access to drinking water, thanks to its availability, throughout the country
- Senegalese social and economic actors (service providers) who will benefit from all necessary good-quality water (plenty of water supply on time within the country) critical to their operations.

Expected Results :

- Long term Results :

  Permanent availability of fresh water all over CAEC arid lands.
  Build all the necessary infrastructures related to the production and transportation of fresh water, after sea water desalinization operated on three sites (Kribi, Huambo, Lobito)
  Re-vegetate the CAEC sahelian area with fruit trees
  Make aquaculture industry possible by injecting small doses of fresh water on a daily basis, along the Chad river
  Selling fresh water is income generating
  A sustainable financing (a 25/30 years loan) that will be paid thanks to the sale of fresh water
  Extend the project to South Africa and to East Africa

- Middle term results :

  CEEAC, will be equipped with a tool to solve the arduous problem of supplying the whole area with fresh and drinkable water.
  CEEAC, will benefit from a powerful tool that will enable the community to efficiently reduce poverty level and enable the area to be emergent.

With this projectfollowing results should be obtained :

- Diagnose the needs for fresh and drinking water ;
- Identify existing infrastructures, access, production capacities, production and collection of useful information related to types of infrastructures needed to achieve the defined objectives ;
- Develop criteria for eligibility of the desalinization, see which network layout should be chosen for water storage sites ;
- Determinate system costs and financial engineering as well as expand the on-site logistics ;
- Support the development of the management project.

Sunugal & Africa' Digest, written and formatted, for each project, for NAICCE & MATICIA, according to RSE tools and methods –   Free Document

3

115

RESPONSIBLE SOLUTION PROPOSED

The lenghty stoppage in water supplies in urban areas, the lack of water in the countryside and the increase in need due to the rapid development growth are a severe impediment to the development of the CAEC countries.

Water shortage in the Sahelo-Sahelian area remains the main cause for poverty, famine and internal conflicts.

This study is implemented in order to examine the feasibility of FRESH WATER PRODUCTION AND TRANSPORTATION THROUGHOUT CAEC COUNTRIES FOLLOWING SEA WATER DESALINISATION.

This study will highlight opportunities induced by the increase of irrigated lands, on site water consumption and transportation

This study will enable an enlightened opinion in quality control laboratory and potential agrobusiness industries. The legal issue will also be considered while launching the private company, to secure the reimbursement process.

1. 4. BENEFICIARIES AND ACTORS

- The Government endowed to implement this project in order to increase production, transportation and distribution of fresh water throughout the country
- Farmers and the whole industry concerned need to increase the number of qualified staff in order to get better results
- In order to support this project, the state will be intentional about building capacity of all the persons with management duties and available staff in activities related to production, transportation and distribution of fresh water ;
- Both farmers and service providers will be supervised, in order to work in conformity with the referential rules according to the international standards.

Project Management :

The state approach being based on deficiencies and the necessity to get to development, the Project will be managed by a designated expert from CLUB SENEGAL EMERGENT and MATICIA, with the help of the concerned ministry officials.

Cost, duration and financing program of the Project studies:

The six-months cost estimation of the Project to be implemented is one million euros, with two expected workshops, the first one will validate the mid-term report, and a subregional workshop will validate the final report of the project.

Sunugal & Africa' Digest, written and formatted, for each project, for NAICCE & MATICIA, according to RSE tools and methods –   Free Document

4

116

SUSTAINABLE OPPORTUNITY

This project is a sustainable answer to the need of the population for fresh drinking water, with the opportunity given by bringing fresh water to the arid lands inside Africa.

The point is to validate the production of plenty of fresh water, thanks to the sea water desalinization at a basic cost of 100 FCFA per m3.

There is no reason why Senegal and even Africa should be deprived of such an asset, both environmental, and affordable.

Economic Incidence of the project in African

The implementation of facilities for production, transportation and distribution of fresh water throughout CAEC country will allow different actors of the agricultural sector to offer a high quality production at very competitive price

The availability of fresh drinking water is going to critically improve populations health level and favour income generating activities.

By doing so, the authorities will be able, on a permanent basis, to maintain the skills required according to international standards in order to ensure food safety, and rebuild a climate of confidence among populations, enjoying fresh drinking water everyday.

The production/transportation and distribution of fresh drinking water is the perfect social and economic integration tool in Africa

TECHNOLOGY BREACH & COMPETITIVE SITUATION

There will be no reason to make a review of technical characteristics and a competitive performance indicator of technological maturity, for all the equipment and material are already in the public domain and have already been a well-proven seller for years (Israël, Morocco)

There still is no or limited competition considering the investment, the nature of the work to be done, the volume to be produced (transportation and delivery) on remote sites.

Sunugal & Africa' Digest, written and formatted, for each project, for NAICCE & MATICIA, according to RSE tools and methods -   Free Document

5

117

ASSETS, DATES & KEY FIGURES

April May and June July to December 2019	1. Transmission of letter of intent of the Project . 2. Preparation of documents: Project Introduction Document, Business Plan, Booklet with the list of the various jobs, etc. 3. Financing Engineering, with the accounting, legal, patrimonial and fiscal condition 4. Research of financial partners for fundraising
2020 2021 2022	9. Construction starting date: construction of sea water desalinization and installation of new pipes 10.Economic development according to identified level of growth qualified by these new clients 11. Project Launch Phase II and phase III

The estimated global cost of the project at the time of the launch is 875 billions CFA

The management EDDS project is a Limited Liability Company, with a registered capital of 50 million Cfa (Eur 75000), valued on accounting and patrimonial condition to EUR 200 000, with 100 % retained by the funding members and primary business partners.
The social share is worth EUR 30

MARKET SEGMENTS

The market of supplies offered by EDDS presents a number of opportunities as regards:
- a quasi-state monopoly of fresh water producers
- a political will to ensure and increase the level and quality of fresh water in order to meet the increasing needS of the populations.
- a high profitability whatever price targeted services are sold and regardless of the financial gains (the law of averages) on the market.
- the sustainable loan proposed to be refunded in an average time of 30 and 50 years.

Except for Senegal, the project starting point, all the East African countries (Sudan, Ethiopia, Egypt) are potentially liable for the development of similar activities

STATES & GOVERNMENT + NGO'S
LOCAL TERRITORIAL COLLECTIVITIES
NATIONAL WATER DISTRIBUTION COMPANY AND NEW PRIVATE COMPANIES
MANAGEMENT OF SENEGAL & NIGER RIVERS
PRIVATE LANDOWNERS

With these 5 identified and professional market segments, means to implement the targeted objectives are thus upgraded.

Senegal & Africa' Digest, written and formatted, for each project, for NAICCE & MATICIA, according to RSE tools and methods -   Free Document

6

SIMPLIFIED PREVISIONAL OPERATION KEY FIGURES

Bank statement in CFA franc

Loan : 875
Loan duration : 30 years
Compensation rate : 6 %
Annuity :

Yearly Production : 365 000 000 m^3
Unit cost for 1m^3 : 100 FCFA
Annual income : 36,5

Items		Yearly Amount (billions CFA)	Yearly Totals (billions CFA)
Total expenses		31,5	31,5
(Loan refund	30		
Including operational costs)	1,5		
Total Income		36,5	36,5
Margin		5	5

Figures on 30 years

	Item	Yearly amount (billion CFA)	Total on 30 years (billion CFA)
	Loan Refund	30	900
Expenses	Operational Cost	1,5	45
	Total expenses	31,5	945
Income	Total income	36,5	1095
Margin	Gross Margin	5	110

LEVEL OF GROWTH & CAPITAL INCREASE

April May & June 2019	5000 euros Fund raising for the purchase of one unit of equipment needed to start activity
July to December 2019	10 000 euros Fund raising for the purchase of 05 units needed to start activity in 05 additional countries
2020 2021 2022	02 million euros to launch Kinshasa Business Club

Sunugal & Africa' Digest, written and formatted, for each project, for NAICCE & MATICIA, according to RSE tools and methods.-   Free Document

7

119

4. The search engine with African content

PRIVATE PROJECT

Matatu

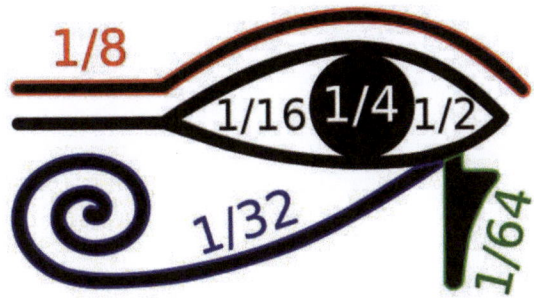

Mail address Maat-Matatu

Mmail ou Maatmail

5. The huge energy potential that needs to be promoted

Abundant and eco-friendly production of Electricity

We are insisting to have this production side included in this project. Time has come for

- Construction of a dam at KOUILOU NSOUNDA and as many as possible other smaller dams
- a deployment of booms, on the Kouilou river and the Congo river
- construction of a gas terminal, in addition to the mineral port to be built (iron mineral export) with storage terminals (12/32/64/500 Gm3, coming from all the countries producing oil within the Gulf of Guinea such as Cameroon, Equatorial Guinea, Gabon, Congo, Angola) with their 10/20/50 gas plants producing 3 to 15 GW

Central Africa needs not to import nuclear danger through unaffordable power plants even for free.

6. On-site refining of African minerals

The once, European economic model that has been existing since the 19th century, is presently an outdated technology due to :

- unaffordable production costs due to the transportation length
- high and negative environmental impact as far as duration and distance are concerned
- poor economic benefits in extracting countries
- the new generation political will to get the most for the continent

Blast furnaces installation

Zambia already refines locally 20% of its copper and intends to get to 50 % of its products locally refined in 5-years time.

The states of Congo and Gabon can't but do better, as they already have great assets to be added to this, in comparison with Zambia :

- Possibility of sharing funds with Gabon for the installation of blast furnaces that shall be used by both to get their iron extracts refined on closer sites
- Possibility to supply locally produced electrical power to blast furnaces (less than 100 km from them) that will be abundant, eco-friendly, and affordable;
- Possibility of installation of mills and steel factories, following iron production
- Installation of iron and steel-based industries, within 150 km from mineral extracting sites

Rough sketches of blast furnaces to keep in mind

Blast Furnace (BF) Facilities

Hopper Down comer

Charging conveyor
Coke
Pellet
Sintered ore
Iron ore

Large bell
Stock line

Throat

Gas cleaner Hot stove

Shaft

Hot blast
Hot blast main

Bustle pipe Belly
Bosh

BF gas

Slag taphole

Slag
Hot metal

1,420K
1,520K

Blast

Exhaust gas

Tuyere

Slag car   Taphole

Torpedo car

Operation principle

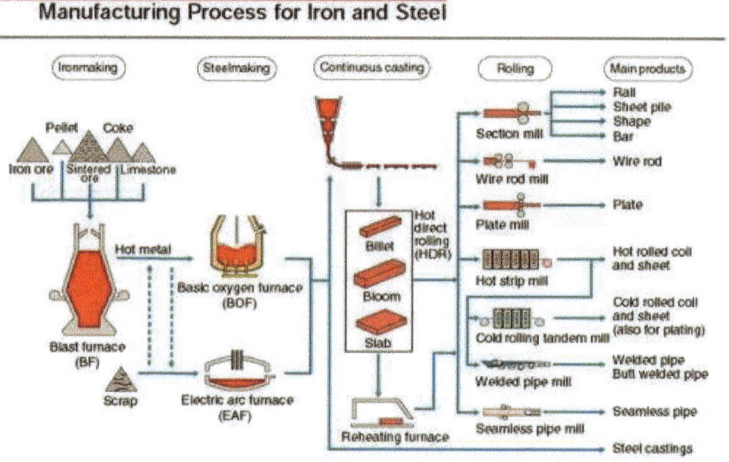

Manufacturing Process for Iron and Steel

126

Benefits in terms of urbanization

The urban zone case situated within 150 km, from the City Council of Pointe Noire

Undoubtedly the SAPRO-MAYOKO Project is going to become the backbone of New Pointe Noire 2 with its mineral terminal added to is gas terminal.

The main objective is to build a new city, focused on the new airport.

The most elegant and most expensive seaside villas will be built in this neighborhood.

Tramway railways (100 km) will be built to join the new city to the old Pointe Noire.

The new airport will be the nest (nzita dia nzâ) around which the new city of Pointe Noire will be built, including new neighborhoods (Nsi Mona, Bouala Tchipoutou, Cabinda, Bouiti, Lubinou, Bouatchi, Tchimakeka, Kakamoeka, highways (Diosso/Dolisie connecting to Hinda), its electric railroad on the third bridge across Kouilou river and modern facilities (universities, malls, international conference centers, luxury hotels.

The following objective is to supply the 150 km wide urban area of Pointe Noire, a 3,000 m long certified airplane runway, like Brazzaville, Ollombo and Ouesso, so that every type of plane will be able to land easily.

The project of the new airport "Tchissanga"nzita"

Characteristics

Runway

Length: 4000/4500 m

Width : 60 m

Roadside: 7,5 m

Stopway: 250 (within two lines)

Reservation: 250 m (within two lines)

Orientation: 17/35 (to be confirmed according to stronger winds on-site)

Connections

Four, on the north

- Two in the lines at 90°
- One at 2500 m, inclination 60°, exit to the right, AMV direction
- One at 1500 m, inclination 60°, exit to the right, AMV direction

Four, on the south

- Two in the lines at 90°
- One at 3500 m, inclination 60°, exit to the right, non-AMV direction
- One at 2000 m, inclination 60°, exit to the right, non-AMV direction

Circulation ways

One way circulation 4,000 m northside

One way circulation southside

Runway light

Highlighted HI/BI with tracers

Daylight, road marking, and fluorescent panels

Energy

Normal/Emergency (multisource, wind power, solar, GE, city sector)

Waste Water Treatment (waste or surface water)

Wastewater Reservoir processed to resist erosion

Wastewater and recycling plant

The project of the new city of Pointe Noire

city systemization

What about the new airport around the nest (nzita dia nzâ)

the neighborhood

 Bouala Tchipoutou, Cabinda, Bouiti Lubinou, Bouatchi, Tchimakeka, Kakamoeka

Highways

airport /Diosso: 40 km

airport/Dolisie: 150 km along the new railway

airport/Hindi: 15 km

Madingou Kayes/Mayumba (Gabon) Madingou Kayes/Mayumba(Gabon), 250 km including the bridge over La Noumbi and the seaside villas (boualatchimputu)

Electric power trains on 120 km, Madingou Kayes/Diosso

The third bridge built over Kouilou river added to modern facilities (U'Tamsi university, malls, international conference center and, luxury hotels).

7. The 50,000 km railway system to be built

Starting from the nest (Brazzaville and Kinshasa, to link all the capital cities of East Africa (Ndjamena, Bangui, Yaounde, Libreville, Pointe Noire, Luanda, Bujumbura, Kigali, Juba).

This multidirectional project will allow to

- Realize railroads electrification by using our potential energy produced by hydroelectrical dams, gas terminals etc.
- Drawing of new railway lines, construction of electric lines, new railway stations etc., are included in the present project. These new lines being :
- North-West line, 3,600 km; Kinshasa/Bandundu/Lisala/GBadolite/Zongo
- North-East line, 4,000 km; Kinshasa/Bokungu/Kisangani/Bonalia/Buta/Juba
- East line, 3,500 km; Kinshasa/Kananga/Kindu/Bukavu/Goma/Kigali
- South line, 3,500 km; Kinshasa/Kenge/Kikwit/Tchikapa/Kamina/Lubumbashi
- West line, 600 km; Kinshasa/Brazzaville/Pointe Noire via bridge-railway
- South-West line, 1,500 km; Kinshasa/Luanda

For Central Africa alone, 50,000 km of railroads need to be built; for the rest of Africa there is a need for about 100,000 km of railroads. This gives Africa an opportunity for a partnership with China and/or/Japan, for mounting and assembly or engines and train wagons, near Mayoko and Owendo refining sites

8. The Kaolack Gas Terminal Project in Senegal at Kaolack

Infrastructures

LNG Side

- High-tonnage vessels Terminal with a capacity of one ship every other day.

- LGN Storage yards du GNL with a capacity of 16 to 32 Gm_3

- Gas powers with a capacity of 300 MW each, which will be producing 3 to 6 GW

- West Africa HT/THT connecting lines for the selling process

- LGN domestic bottling plants

- Industrial gases plants

- Sea water desalination and pipe conveyors plants on 1000 km, with installation of optical fiber, in order to connect university poles

- Urban waste treatment and recycling

Classic terminals side

- Containers Terminal with a capacity of one ship every other day

Target Objectives

- Creation of the second deep water terminal in Senegal

- Have sufficient LGN reserves from 16 to 32 Gm$_3$

- Production of electricity with a capacity of 3 to 6 GW

- Bottle filling and domestic and industrial gas commercialization

- Desalinated water Production, transportation and selling

- Increase in transit shipping volumes

9. The Gas Terminal of Pointe-Noire, Congo

Infrastructures

LNG Side

- High tonnage Methane vessel terminal with a capacity of one vessel every other day
- LNG storage yards with a capacity of 16 to 32 Gm3
- 300 MW gas plants with a production of 5 to 10 GW
- Central Africa HT/THT network line for selling use
- LNG Bottling factories for domestic use ; industrial gas factories
- Seawater Desalinization plants with transportation to arid lands
- Optical fibre installation for the connection of university poles
- Waste and recycling plants

Classical terminals side

Terminals equipped with containers for the processing of a vessel every other day

Targeted Objectives

. Launching the second deep water port in Congo

.Benefit from LNG reserves (16 to 32 Gm3)

. Electricity production (5 to 10 GW to be sold by THT/HI lines to be built

. Bottling and commercialization of domestic and industrial gas

. Freshwater production by seawater desalinization including sales and transportation oater

.Increase of the goods in transit.

10. The University Centres

Infrastructures

- Construction of 2 university poles for each country, which makes 30 poles

- There will be various faculties/schools with a 10,000 places boarding school and lodgings for the teachers

- a fully-equipped MEDICAL CENTER, (MRI machine, scanner, medical staff...), as all the students will be covered by a universal health insurance

- Each pole will be connected to Fresh water, Electricity and optical fiber networks going through all member states

Target Objectives

- Produce a significant increase in the number of infrastructures to generate a knowledge-based economy in the USOA area

- Increase the number of university numbers within the Union

- Create places to boost intellectual and scientific activity (the intelligentsia melting-pot)

- Create consumption points for the abundant agricultural

Production due to the presence of fresh water that can be found everywhere up to arid lands in the USOA.

- Bring 10 % of the exiled students back by providing them

With costless quality education, nearby the Union countryside.

- Give them a valuable type of social integration

Through students and teachers exchange between all the universities within the Union

- Finance research and support innovative programs, as well as marketing technologies

11. The Congo River Festival, cultural link

This project named THE RIVER CONGO PROJECT means to consolidate the cultural links between all the people living along the river.

This project is about :

- The installation of control equipment for the circulation on the 4,500 km long Congo river including its navigable tributaries
- Installation of mills to bring electricity produced and operate on the river high flow rate
- Installation of multi sources electric charging stations
- Deploying CORs equipment, GNSS services, MTO data
- Construction and repairs of secondary river ports
- Deploying of digital terminal for medical consultation
- Etc.
- Launching of the yearly festival of the Congo River, that will be lasting for 10 years (15-25 may). A cultural event during which proverbs will be cited and drums beaten from Kinshasa to Kisangani 'and Bôlôbô to Gemena, and Mandombe/at the estuary of Luwozi).

This idea has been initialized by the History ResearcherArsene Francoeur NGANGA, dedicated to enhance the existing cultural links between people living along the River Congo (traditions, proverbs, habits and customs) songs, music.

12. The contribution of the aviation industry to the integration of the continent

African air transport has been facing many challenges for decades

	Challenges	Projects to be improved
1	Weaknesses in the number of countries covered	Project of leasing and planes maintenance within the continent to favor the creation of air companies
2	Security and safety level	Connecting airports and terminals equipped with facial recognition softaware New X control for luggages equipped with a tracing system effective from departure to arrival
3	Infrastructures below ICAO norms	Project to have properly equipped secondary aerodromes Project Bringing up airports to international standards

	Challenges	Projects to be improved
4	Lack of qualified staff	Training program for DAC staff
5	Air transportation liberalization within the African continent	A Survival plan of the national structures in view of this liberalization
6	Free access to the market	Adapt existing legislation to the opening of the African air transport
7	Complete traffic rights concerning 1st, 2nd, 3rd, 4th and, possibilities of service	Adapt existing legislation to the opening of the African air transport

As far as challenges are concerned, one can see a flaw in countries covering that do not meet international standards, a poor level of infrastructures that do not meet ICAO standards, and the lack of qualified staff.

Since 1970, the Bank of African Development works to meet these challenges, by financing 49 operations related to air transport, including the building of 14 new airports, rehabilitation or reconstruction of 19 airports (including equipment installation for navigational aid=.

Central Africa is one of the most poorly equipped as far as the world and African air transport is concerned.

Facilitation of the flow of people and goods is a ZLEC policy meant to increase the mobility for 440 million people living in West and Central Africa.

These two areas producers of perishable goods of great added value (fish, vegetable, flowers) which need to be sent by cargo planes to industrialized countries.

Africa is a real opportunity, the continent of the future for humanity, in which everything good is happening, the desirable future, the path of grow. Here is some examples:

- Open market of air transportation sector for 55 states covering 30 million square kilometers.
- Creation of leasing facilities for Boeing and Airbus
- Launching of maintenance warehouse for A, B, C and, D plane types named FUNZU NZINGA, thanks to the installation of black furnaces for iron refining concerted to steel, at the world's lower cost because the proximity of extraction sites and, an abundant production of electricity at the best possible purchase price.

Possibilities of the continent as far as civil aviation is concerned

1.implementing projects of a sky for all in Africa Airspace

"Connecting and operational networking" throughout all Africa for Air Navigation Services suppliers.

The first step to a common airspace is dialogue between all ANS Providers existing in the continent, at technical level.

Both ASECNA and ATNS have launched a common program to be extended to others (Nigeria, Angola, RD Congo, Maghreb)

Project for equipment of secondary aerodromes within all African countries

Project of training and capacity development of DAC staff

Clear the backlog concerning air security engendered by the lack of equipment existing in most of African secondary aerodromes

Properly trained DAC's staff to reduce lack of competences

Second step

The Project for a satellite covering the African aerospace telecommunication

The Project for the use of optical fiber to connect all the African airports

A common project for a satellite networking in Africa for all the aerospace telecommunication

A common satellite + the Nigerian N° 1 emergency satellite + Angola N° 2 emergency satellite

The optical fiber interconnection satellite, as emergency equipment N° 3 for the continent airports

FUNZU NZINGA rocket launch pad or aerospace industry for Africa

Iron and aluminum mineral extraction situated at 300 km (Mayoko, Owendo, Mfouati) from the launch pad

Refining plants for iron, aluminum and gold close to extraction sites

Production of available and abundant eco-friendly electricity, close to the launch pad (500 km)

1200 MW from Kouilou Sounda,3000 MW from 10 gas terminals 2GW from INGA III

Steel-based industries

Satellites Manufacture

An African Training center in TIBESTI, Faya Largeau and Saraya/Kedougou (Senegal)

2. A project for the opening of aerial transport market in Africa

A project of optical fiber based interconnection for the airports within the continent

Safety and Security Data sharing

Supply and installation of luggage control with new X control facilities including passengers' luggage labelling and facial recognition equipment

A project for GNSS Satellite Navigation equipment

This facility applies to all types of transportation and implementation has already been approved by African Union

A project for planes leasing

A certified center of maintenance for planes

A funding plan for planes leasing in the continent

A project for planes insurance in the continent

This planes market (leasing, maintenance, insurance, financial support) make us very optimistic in terms of development, especially as planes insurance is concerned in Africa

A project for the modification of the concerned countries legislation to validate the opening of this market in Africa

The writing of a common legislation, by adding related point disseminated in every state to facilitate and harmonize the air traffic in the continent by taking out the excessive bureaucracy for which DAC are often known

A project for the building of additional commercial infrastructures

for Maya, there is a need for airport extension, airport village and facilities for airport emergencies for Agostino Neto, the freight zone, hydrants and the emergency facilities

to increase the revenue from ground handling of the concession

the tariff of Air services dealers will need to be scaled down to reduce air ticket prices in the continent

Refining sites Project for all countries producing oil

Kerosene remains very expensive operational costs for air companies

With their refining sites African oil producers will be able to supply fuel at an affordable price (-21%)

A project of a passport with no visa required for African people (acted on March 21th 2018 at Kigali)

Free Moving - Free Seating – Free Trading

No visa for Africans or a single passport for Africa

A condition for free circulation of persons and goods in ZLEC

3. **Flight simulator available in the 55 existing aeroclubs of the continent**

4. **Flight Training Schools built near the plain maintenance centers**

5. **A Project of a private meteorological institute for countries around Congo (prived university),**

Including agricultural meteorology center and all relevant branches connected to Libreville Spatial Agency

6. **A project for jobs related to air transportation institute near the planes leasing pole**

7. **A project for airport emergency facilities including medical airlift fleet**

13. Plan KRUMAH for Africa: the backbone of the African Federal State

Items	Actions Taken	Receipts and Amount
Fresh Drinking water	Installation of seawater desalinization plants 5 units of 200 000 cubic meter per site 20 sites (Nouadhibou, Nouakchott, Saint Louis Kaolack, Ziguinchor.....) Transportation of freshwater from the sea to arid lands Selling freshwater to refund loan Planting of vegetable and fruit trees to ensure food security Implement agro-food industries to enable preservation of fruit and vegetables	Fight famine, drought, Poverty and, conflicts in Africa 94 billion euros to be raised throughout Africa as a long-term loan (50 years)
Urban Waste	Installation of collection centers for the treatment and recycling of urban waste, spilled in rivers and oceans	A private business whose investments may be covered by selling recycled products and citizen contribution (one dollar every two month per capita)

Items	Actions Taken	Receipts and Amount
Electric Energy	Production of abundant, and affordable eco-friendly electricity Hydro-electric dams (Inga III, Kouilou Sounda, Kasaï I & II) Installation of hydrokinetic equipment along the two Congo river banks (4000 km long) Production of electricity, through LNG, 3 to 5 GW for each producer country Installation of HT/THT distribution /transportation/sale electricity lines for Africa	30 billion euros Profitability obtained through electricity sale By using PPA payable in advance,
Locally Refined minerals prior to export	Installation of blast furnaces, steel plants and mills in the area between Owendo (Gabon) and Mayoko (Congo) near mineral extraction sites	Locally produced to encourage the implantation of steel-based industries

Items	Actions Taken	Receipts and Amount
Railroad to be installed	First phase: linking Malebo Pool (Brazzaville and Kinshasa) to all the CAEC capital cities (Libreville, Brazzaville, Bangui, Ndjamena, Juba, Kigali, Bujumbura, Lusaka, Luanda); up to 100 000 km of railroads Second phase: rally Dakar to Addis Abbaba, including stop stations at Bamako, Ouagadougou, Niamey, Diffa, Maïduguri, Ndjamena, Juba with connections to Ziguinchor, Bissau, Conakry, Abidjan, Lome, Cotonou, Lagos	Train wagons and railways will be imported from China to begin with Then, the plan is to have them manufactured equipment on the continent between Congo and Gabon, following the iron plant, mills and steel plants to be built nearby the extraction sites The eco-friendly Electricity that will be locally produced and sold at affordable price should allow the lowest sales price worldwide

Items	Actions Taken	Receipts and Amount
All electric transportation Industry in Africa	Introducing electric car wagons and trains, beginning in 2020, in ZLEC area, and economic asset and a challenge for fighting against air pollution.	
Trains, cars, boats, cabs and, drones	Manufacturer could introduce licensed Renault Zoe cars, then develop their model, at machining cost 5000/6000 euro, following the organization of distribution network for the supply of vehicle spare parts, collection of used batteries, installation of multi-source refill stations in the continent	
	The third generation of vehicles will be locally available for the vehicles should be manufactured in the continent due mineral refining sites and the abundance of electricity	
	The taxi drones are to be included following the official statements of law and rules related to their use as aircrafts according to civil aviation	
	Under-equipped Africa will get rid of fossile fuel models as soon as proper partnership will be available	

Items	Actions Taken	Receipts and Amount
Civil Aviation business in ZLEC	China has ordered 150 Airbuses for domestic use, Africa can acquire 100 additional Airbuses to use within the continent. A maintenance workshop will be built in Africa to this end The management of African airports concessions will be upgraded with adequate passengers control equipment (interconnection of African airports and data sharing with real time border crossing information Satellite orbiting phase would enable to combine African ANS PROVIDERS to scale down aeronautical charges	Africa represents an opportunity because of the opening of the aerial transportation market and the implementation of one sky in Africa

153

Items	Actions Taken	Receipts and Amount
The knowledge And Digital economy	China will have to train at least 55 000 African students, during 5 years (one thousand for each country), to compensate the growing deficit in technical areas, Suffered by Africa	Knowledge transfer and technology knowledge Will be paired to environmental knowledge
	Efforts will be made to build 5 to 10 university poles for each African country to help African stay at home	
	Key university poles such as those covering all the fields related to meteorology or related to the preservation of the forest ecosystems will be prioritized.	
	All African cities will be supplied with optical fiber equipment and refund will be ensured through private management	

Items	Actions Taken	Receipts and Amount
The Preservation Of Forest ecosystems	The presence of water will enable the reforestation of Savannas and arid lands Only trees that have been planted in the first place will be allowed to be cut down to meet the industrial needs Natural forests may never be cut down to preserve the forest ecosystems With the help of Canada and China one may develop aquaculture, along the continent littoral Laboratories specialized in sowing species will take into account the overconsumption of some species to help in the management of farm fish (saltwater fish and freshwater fish)	From now on, it is urgent to clean our planet, recycle urban and toxic waste and begin the reforestation process as well as sowing the most endangered species in the sea

Items	Actions Taken	Receipts and Amount
Building gold reserve for Africa	A call for public and private savings, through a private initiative, to encourage a personal contribution from each African citizen by buying one (1) dollar worth shares, a day during 10 years. The gold reserve will be gathered to the minimum amount of 10 thousand tons for each gold producer country , which amount to 50 000 tons for 5 countries.	

Dedication

To

Simon KIBAMGU, who died in prison because he stand to the truth by saying that we are all human and that Black people and White people should live in brotherhood

To Black people of Africa, summoned to free themselves from moral and mental servitude, from unbridled pursuit of earthy goods, and to build their continent, the desirable future for humanity

And Also to

YÄH NEGHOST, Anzimba from Akoua community who has become a better man

MAME HULO GUILLABERT, for her involvement in the Pan Africanist movement, Mame Africa

CLAUDE ARTHUR LEWONA, for the discussion on the world globality

CHLOE DE BANGUI, born ZOUGARANI NGOMBET

Bibliography

Article Wikipédia

- Le nombre et la spirale, d'Or
- USA Constitution
- Anthem to Aton

From the same author

- **Business Intelligence in Africa,**
Edilivre Mai 2018

- **France, with its plural identity and mixed cultured, a world champion,**
Edilivre, sept 2019

- **L'avenir désirable de l'humanité. L'Afrique,**
Editions Diasporas noires, 2019

- **The desirable future of humanity. Africa,**
Edition Diasporas noires, 2019

- **Global Change in NgalaKongo,**
Edilivre, mai 2019